An Exile on Planet Earth

An Exile on Planet Earth

Articles and Reflections

Brian Aldiss

Bodleian Library
UNIVERSITY OF OXFORD

First published in 2012 by the Bodleian Library
Broad Street
Oxford OX1 3BG

www.bodleianbookshop.co.uk

ISBN: 978 1 85124 373 0

'Metaphysical Realism' is a revised version of an article which first appeared in *Science Fiction Studies*, vol. 114, July 2011.

'Hothouse' first appeared as an Afterword to the Penguin 2008 edition of the novel, *Hothouse*.

'A Sight of Serbian Churches' first appeared in *The Norman Arch,* 2002.

'It's the Disorientation I Relish' is from Brian Aldiss's introduction to *A Science Fiction Omnibus*, edited by Brian Aldiss, London, 2007 (pp. vii–xii). Introduction © Brian Aldiss. Reproduced by permission of Penguin Books Ltd.

'The Gulag Archipelago' was first published in 2005 by The Folio Society as an Introduction to their edition of Aleksandr Solzhenitsyn's book *The Gulag Archipelago.*

'The Continuing War of the Worlds' is from Brian Aldiss's introduction to the Penguin Classics edition of *The War of the Worlds* by H.G. Wells, London, 2005 (pp. xiii–xxix). Introduction © Brian Aldiss. Reproduced by permission of Penguin Books Ltd.

'Meeting Thomas Hardy' was first published in Editor Dale Salwak's *AfterWord: Conjuring the Literary Dead*. Reprinted with the permission of the University of Iowa Press, 2011.

Cover design by Dot Little

Design and typeset in Perpetua (14pt on 17.1pt) by JCS Publishing Services Ltd, www.jcs-publishing.co.uk

Printed and bound by MPG Books Group Ltd

British Library Catalogue in Publishing Data
A CIP record of this publication is available from the British Library

Contents

Acknowledgements

I wish to acknowledge the help and friendship I have had over many years from Dr Judith Priestman in particular, and from Dr Samuel Fanous, Dr Christopher Fletcher and Clive Hurst, as well as that paragon, Bodley's Librarian, Dr Sarah E. Thomas.

Publisher's Note

This book is published to celebrate the deposit of the main Brian Aldiss archive in the Bodleian Library.

Foreword

I first encountered Brian Aldiss in the pages of his fiction, as an impressionable student in the late sixties, but it was only with the passage of time that I began to be aware of the scope of his literary ambition: not just a master of science fiction, but a poet, an editor and an anthologist too, with the kind of imagination and curiosity which could get you into a lot of trouble if you weren't a professional author of a certain age and thus obliged to stay at home and write. Nevertheless, I have to acknowledge that when I first met Brian in the flesh in his charming Oxford cottage down a quiet country lane I was a tad disappointed not to find an alien nesting in the garden. This is, after all, a man who has ranged more planets and epochs (and of course written more books in his eight-plus decades) than most of us have had cups of tea.

It was spring of 2008 and I had come to film Brian for an *Imagine* programme I was making about his long-time friend and fellow author, the formidable Doris Lessing. He didn't disappoint. His recall was spot on, with an eye for the telling detail which is apparent in these essays, and a mischievous sense of humour which kept us all entertained.

In these essays, fruit of a lifetime's explorations, he looks back. Both the productivity and the plots spring, he now realizes, from the subconscious realization that his mother never loved him. This was consolidated by years spent at boarding school, and then abroad in the Far East, enforcing that outsider aloofness. There is a loneliness and a searching in his seventy-plus books – which can *not*, by the way, be pigeonholed as 'science fiction'. As Brian says, 'people have always enjoyed science fiction when that label is removed.' He and his friend C.S. Lewis used to call it 'speculative fiction' – 'the term science fiction was considered too plebeian.' What he gives us here is the reality that underlies the fiction: personal stories, often of pain, that illuminate the work.

Some of these essays evoke another world, not on another planet, but in our own past: a world of Green Shield stamps, florins, counterpanes and communism. He looks back, as he does at the former Yugoslavia – and especially at the churches he found flourishing there – with 'something like regret'.

He reflects here, too, upon science fiction. 'As an academic remarked to me, "I'm not interested in the machinery, it's the disorientation that I relish."' It's the 'disarray of the soul' (James Tiptree Jr's phrase), with which Aldiss admits to having 'nodding acquaintance', and a discontent with the world-as-is which fire his writing.

Foreword

'We are the Steppenwolves of our culture': Steppenwolves, that is, who come into society from outside, perfectly harmless but always critical.

Fantasy, he says, tends to end happily – 'a conservative ending'. In science fiction, the world will never be the same again. And that revolutionary quality is what he values in it, and what I find in his writing. As he puts it here: 'imagination, and its cousin ingenuity. We should grant it more respect.' Indeed we should, and then the world never *would* be the same again.

He once told me, 'When I first sort of joined the science fiction club, people were claiming that it saw the future and was prophetic. I don't think that's the case at all. I think it's actually an analogy for something that is already happening.' An analogy, yes, but with a glorious freedom to spiral off and away. As he said to me, 'you devise a different world for yourself.'

He also gave me a more down-to-earth reason for not liking the science fiction writer label: 'I'm perfectly content with what I've done and at first I was very glad to have that umbrella, but it's like being a crime writer or a sports writer; if there's an adjective in front of writer you're less. You're less than you were if you were just a writer.'

Here we find some brilliant observations and the kind of detail that will delight aficionados of his fiction: 'Cultivating the wilderness, it's what a writer does all the while. What we are fills the fictions we tell, often without our realizing it. What one pours out, alone in the room, is much like sessions of psychoanalysis, as one produces things that astonish even oneself.' For those revelations this is a book well worth reading.

Alan Yentob

1

Metaphysical Realism

Metaphysical Realism

The psychiatrist Anthony Storr has written of a psychological theory which holds the key to my understanding of why I write. In his book, *The Dynamics of Creation*, Storr writes, 'A child could have experiences of pleasure and pain which he could never consciously recall, but which, from this deep level, continue to influence him.' Whatever the truth of that may be, we do seem to contain some kind of un-get-at-able self within us. And to get at it can become a preoccupation. And even lead to the writing of science fiction.

Many people are mystified as to why writers write. If you write crime novels or murder mysteries, then I suppose the motivation is primarily to make money. That apart, why undergo such extensive labours, often ignored by popular critics and non-diligent readers alike?

The answer, or the pursuit of an answer, amounts in my case to something like seventy hardcover books and many other books of all kinds, poetry, mini-sagas, collections of other writers' stories, selections of essays, and of course my artwork, which speaks – if only in a low mutter – when silence falls. I have been diligent, and enjoyed my long swim in language. But only recently have I washed up on the beaches of Metaphysical Realism. It is a clumsy term but anything is better than that clunking hybrid 'science fiction'. The term was coined by a man from Luxembourg, Hugo Gernsback, who emigrated to the USA to sell wireless sets. He founded a magazine called *Amazing Stories*. The title of one story, 'Moon of Mad Atavism', says it all: a man lands on an alien planet where the atmosphere is such that he de-evolves into a tyrannosaurus. Gernsback called this 'scientifiction', only later upgrading it to 'science fiction'.

Let me explain my Metaphysical Realism.

Some years ago, a friend of mine was editing the Christmas number of *Harper's Bazaar*. He wrote to me saying he urgently needed a short story of about three thousand words.

Without a great deal of cogitation or hesitation, I wrote him a story entitled 'Super-Toys Last All Summer Long'. The story was duly published in the magazine in December 1969, and has since been reprinted several times. In my essay, 'Zulu', later in this volume, I describe how I worked with Stanley Kubrick on a screenplay of the story which, after Kubrick's death, formed the basis of the film *A.I.* directed by Steven Spielberg.

The cadences of that story's title are alluring, seeming on the face of it to promise tranquillity, but underneath lies the unsettling suggestion that summers, however long, can never last. It took a while for the metaphorical implications of this story to dawn on me. It lives as veiled memory for the fact that my mother did not love me: a memory of which I suggest I was unconscious at the time of writing the story.

I am mindful of the Augusts I spent on the beaches of Walcot, Norfolk, as a child. I played alone there all day, deflecting miniature streams, building dams and castles, sprawling in warm miniature lakes, perfectly content. The thread woven through my novel, *Walcot* (2009), a history of the twentieth century as seen through the eyes of one family, the Fieldings, is a question, a conundrum: whether or not little Steve Fielding is left to play alone on the beach all day despite incoming tides because his parents wish to rid themselves of him. This question is raised later in Steve's life by a rather unreliable aunt. He struggles to resolve it – the moral being that in most of our complex lives there are riddles we cannot solve. An alien is present throughout the entire story, unannounced; this is metaphysical science fiction.

The year is now 2010. I have finished writing a novel entitled *Finches of Mars*. I accept an invitation to address a readers' book club in Summertown, Oxford. Eight women are sitting round a table laden with flowers, pleasant light food, and wine. My readers are academics or wives of academics, I imagine. All read and enjoy science fiction, while not being interested in hard science. They enjoy the speculation and the futurescapes. The enjoyment comes from a transposition of real life into an unreal one. Real life is challenging enough; the unreal has its enticements. They don't talk of sci-fi.

People have always enjoyed SF when that label is removed. In the earlier decades of the eighteenth century, Jonathan Swift wrote *Gulliver's Travels*. Not long afterwards came Daniel Defoe's *Robinson Crusoe*. For two centuries these books were unfailingly popular. *Gulliver* is about aliens, or people of different sizes, while *Crusoe* is about a man abandoned on an alien island. I do not use the word 'fantasy'; fantasy is too easy. The kind of novel we are thinking of has its initial posit, and that should be firmly adhered to – no sudden ghosts appear to help out with the storytelling.

So at the book club I abandon the sort of stuff I had planned I might talk to them about. Instead we have a conversation, all joining in. *Walcot* is not about me; Steven, for instance, spends time in the Second World War stuck in a forest in occupied France and later soldiers in the harsh winter of the Ardennes, in the final stages of hostilities, whereas I fought in Burma and Sumatra.

One of the women at the table asks about the tranquil opening of *Walcot*, with the boy on the beach playing there alone all day. Did no one look after him? And suddenly I see the danger I had been in, long ago, totally unsupervised on those sands, which were regularly swallowed at high tide. Yes, when opening the story I had drawn all but unwittingly on my own vulnerability on that lonely beach.

Later I thought this discovery over.

When I was born in the August of 1925 I was a disappointment. I was a boy. No sooner did I learn a few words than I heard about this perfect little girl, born five years earlier, a girl whose manners were exemplary, whose behaviour was impeccable. Unhappily she had died before her fifth birthday. When I asked to see a photograph of her my mother burst into tears. She could not bear to look at a photograph.

Truth was that no photograph existed. No angelic child existed. Mother's child was stillborn. We lived in the shadow of a cast-iron fantasy. So also Steve Fielding's mother, Mary, lives in thrall to her first child, Valerie, stillborn but in her mind vividly alive and far better behaved than Steve.

As Charles Darwin looked at things and saw them as they really were, so was I now looking clearly at things within my self, hidden from my self. I had known they were lurking there, indeed used them to empower my fiction, yet had never perceived them clearly: they were the smoke, not the bonfire. Is not one function of metaphysics to uncover what is ultimately real, even if one moves into the future to wrestle with it? Is not science fiction ideal for this purpose?

The ultimate clincher lies in *Finches of Mars*. A colony is established there. But the women who go to settle on Mars can deliver only stillborn offspring. Would that in truth be the case? Lighter gravity would not force the bones and ligaments of the foetus to form as on Earth. An American professor, Dr Frank Manning, the co-Director of Maternal Foetal Medicine at the New York Albert Einstein College of Medicine, read my work, praised my originality, and declared that what I had written as occurring on Mars was very likely correct.

So here we hark back to 'Super-Toys' and *Walcot* and others. My mother gave birth to a stillborn daughter, five years before my birth. She did not want a boy. She wanted another girl, a replacement, a living daughter. It was this misery, this hidden indignity, which ultimately served to produce a planet full of the stillborn! At last I grasped one source of my creativity.

My mother imagined that that lifeless baby girl had lived. The belief, the pretence, of its years of life – in reality entirely unlived – consumed her, chilled her mind, froze her heart; and that spectral child made miserable my early years.

Greybeard (1964), too, depicts a desolate world without children. My first wife and I had quarrelled bitterly and she had taken away the children, my beloved and irreplaceable children, to live at the seaside. So my imagined England decays without children, those lanterns that light our days. The population ages. England is gone; there is only wilderness. All my isolation from my earlier years rose up to power my little portable typewriter.

Early in my writing life, I encountered the French *nouveau roman*, or anti-novel, as it became known. I read with rapt attention, or at least endurance, the writings of Michel Butor and Alain Robbe-Grillet. The vital core of these novels seemed to be that nothing happened, or was suspected not to have happened. I wished England had a similar movement, almost puritanical, to quell all those novels of war or murder. So I wrote *Report on Probability A* (1968). Three people watch the activities in a big house, where nothing ever happens. I spiked the narrative with my personal hatred of the way my father spied on me when I was a small boy.

Perhaps my own childhood experience also impels me to Mary Shelley's great novel, *Frankenstein* (and the writing of my own novel, *Frankenstein Unbound*). What particular power does *Frankenstein* exert, so much so that the collected novels of Mary Shelley should be published 150 years after her birth, her teenage novel still being read, parodied, quoted, misinterpreted?

Frankenstein exists somewhere between the Enlightenment and Romanticism. Its stormy force comes from Mary's motherless state. Her mother Mary Wollstonecraft died after giving birth to the baby daughter. The horror but pathos of the creature in the novel lies in its effigy status; it is motherless, serving as a metaphor for Mary's loss. 'I am mischievous because I am miserable,' it declares, thus reversing Christian doctrine. Without this shadow haunting the cognitive process, giving it metaphysical weight, *Frankenstein* would be just a silly horror story, and would never have become a classic.

All of which is not to claim that all my fiction is strewn with such ancient scars. For example, world incidents will seize upon us as something we must deal with, to dramatize or protest. My first science fiction novel was *Non-Stop* (first published in 1958). *Non-Stop* concerns occupants of a starship on a long journey to a distant star. Things have gone wrong somewhere on the trip, and the survivors have come to believe that their imprisoning ship is the entire world. It is only when by accident a shutter flies open that men have a clear view of the real universe. (Of course that is what science is doing for our enclosing world, but the point I wish to make here lies elsewhere.)

Non-Stop was translated and published in Poland, which at that time lay oppressed under Communist domination. My novel rose in popularity to number two in the best-seller list there. Curiosity drove me to Posnan, in Poland. I asked, Why the popularity? They replied, smiling, that they knew *Non-Stop* was a coded reference to their imprisonment in Communism, closing them off from the real world.

Metaphors travel far and fast.

Dark Light Years (1964) was provoked by the activities of a scientist who declared that brain/body-weight ratios in dolphins closely resembled those in human beings; so he then brought a dolphin from its natural element, strapped the poor creature to a laboratory bench, and sank electrodes into its brain. The sheer inhumanity of this human had to be satirized.

10

Another incident is more recent. There have been reports of British forces involved in torture. Long ago, while serving as a soldier in Sumatra, I was witness to such an incident. I and others were horrified by this incident, but the pressures of life were such that it became forgotten. Realizing such cruelty continued, I resolved to write about it. The resultant novel, *Harm* (2007), was published in both the UK and USA and elsewhere in Europe.

Perhaps more ambitiously, *The Squire Quartet* was written to reflect a portrait of our times. Spread between various publishers, the quartet has never been presented as such, as an entire panorama. That I regret, since I regard it as a lively and adventurous exploration of past, present, and future (and to some extent of my time, too). Its full variety could be best appreciated if the volumes were approached as one tousle-haired unit. A later novel, *Super State*, published in 2002, was a slightly surreal look at the EU forty years from now, where there is an excellent restaurant at the top of Everest, androids make a nuisance of themselves and are locked in cupboards overnight, and EU forces invade a small eastern state (as the USA and UK shortly afterwards invaded Iraq).

The influences on a writer's life can be varied but often unacknowledged, and, in my case, part of a healing process. Not until I had turned fifty did I discover a tiny grave bearing my stillborn sister's name, hidden in an unconsecrated part of Dereham churchyard, lying under the chestnut trees. Unconsecrated because, being dead, the infant was never christened. Not only did it not live, it never made it to heaven – at least according to the legends of that day and age.

Stephen Hawking asks in his book on M-theory, *The Grand Design*, 'Do we really have reason to believe that an objective reality exists?' At that moment, as I stood there under the chestnut trees, I had come up against objective reality with a bump.

From all this post-natal upset, I conclude I have been writing not even metaphorical fiction, but Metaphysical Realism. I could not help it!

2

Paradise Square

Paradise Square

Leading off Bonn Square was a street which delivered one into Paradise Square – ironically named, one assumed, when I was washed up there in the 1960s, but a part of Oxford's history.

I felt myself to be a failure. I had spent four years in the Far East, in the British army, and wished I were back there. Britain was an alien land, where I could hardly tell a florin from a half-crown. A marriage into which I had been manoeuvred had failed. It had been a struggle to escape from Kidlington, just outside Oxford, into Oxford itself, where I had bought a house in Victoria Road, Summertown. My first wife, Olive, and I had lived there with our children for only two years before the marriage broke up. When I sold that house, all the money went to my wife. Everything had gone, including my young children, Clive and Wendy. The dinginess of Paradise Square well reflected my feelings of exile and homesickness.

It was here that I began my novel *Greybeard*, a story of a wasteland, the English countryside after an ecological fallout, which leaves the human race sterile and the world devoid of children. For old people there was no amelioration, little to live for, and Oxford itself was divided between two rival fortresses, Balliol and Christ Church. The novel was published in hardcover in 1964 and I dedicated it to Clive and Wendy. In writing it I felt a curious strength. This was my tale and I was telling it but transforming it, and no one would know how it originated. I had been moved to write by grief.

I was broke. I was forty. Now I was looking at Oxford from the bottom up, but being homeless I was not exactly one of *the* homeless. I knew a kindly man called George Halcrow, who rented me one room in his house in Paradise Square, that old crumbling Paradise Square, due shortly for demolition. My room was sunny, and had a shallow bay window which looked out on the square towards the playground of the local primary school. The room rental cost me 7s 6d a week. Working by my window, I could hear the glad cries of the children running out for their break. I had bought a knife, fork and spoon for 1s 6d at Woolworth's. I toasted slices of malt loaf at my gas fire. The cellar under my room served as a laundry; curried steam would rise through my floorboards.

My room was in No. 12, Paradise Square. George owned an Indian and a Chinese restaurant and had bought the building cheaply to house the staff of his two restaurants. The staff had left in disgust at the poor conditions. The back garden was so overgrown it qualified as primal swamp. But I liked to walk there. An old man two doors away kept a flight of pigeons in cages. He let the birds out every morning. The pigeons would fly free, to wheel above Paradise Square before returning home for their rations. This event was splendid, a living metaphor for the human spirit soaring above poverty and its humiliations.

Other sights were less splendid. As inhabitants of the square died or moved away, the council shuttered up their old houses, leaving them to decay. Pavements were cracked and broken. The roadway had potholes like pox marks. Autumn leaves piled up in gutters for the winter. My belief is that those who are down-and-out find such an atmosphere congenial, to be preferred to an array of modern glass and stony-faced offices. But the square was doomed; storm clouds of plans for a future multi-storey car park loomed over it.

Paradise Square had been built in Victorian times as Oxford's unique middle-class environment, a modestly elegant square for those who worked in offices. After the Second World War, it was allowed to go downhill. The middle classes had moved on.

There were some assets which helped the poor living their tumble-down lifestyle. I went, rather timidly at first, to the bathhouse at the top of the square. The bathhouse was run by an ex-army sergeant. You paid – well, it was either 2d or 6d, and were given a clean towel and a new sliver of soap. You then entered a cubicle and could climb into a spotlessly clean bath. I liked it and went there often, for No. 12 had no bathroom.

Other amenities included a Co-op in nearby Gas Street. It was a poor bare shop, with wooden floorboards and dim lighting. The women who served there understood poverty; they would cut you half a small white loaf, or a half of the traditional quarter-pound of butter. I shopped there frequently, guiltily enjoying the novelty of being broke. After all, I was a part of the community.

In those days (1959–72) I was literary editor of the *Oxford Mail* in its broadsheet days, under editor Mark Barrington-Ward. And I was writing short stories. The stories I wrote on a borrowed Hermes typewriter began to sell in the USA. When a cheque came in, I would treat myself to another facility of the neighbourhood, an Indian restaurant called the Cobra, down in St Ebbe's, and owned by the benevolent George Halcrow. George might come into the restaurant and, seeing me sitting there, sign my bill so that I did not have to pay. He would lock the door at about midnight, whereupon the Cobra would become George's sort of club. Tarka dhal and beer would still be served by Ali, and privileged customers from local colleges would enjoy long discussions. These sessions often continued deep into the night. One of the cleverest of those who discussed was Eric Korn, whose name was later to be seen in the *TLS*.

Another resource was Mr Barnes's little grocery store on the corner. Late every evening, Mr Barnes would get on his delivery bike and cycle round, delivering his goods; he had had to dispense with his delivery boy –

Thank you for your order

We hope that you enjoy your books. Our aim is to share new, unusual and almost-forgotten titles with as many fellow readers as possible, at affordable prices. Thanks to our long-standing relationships with hundreds of publishers we are able to pass on discounts of **up to 75% off publishers' prices.**

Refer a Friend and you both receive 20% off your order

Visit your 'My Account' area online to access and share your unique 20% off referral link. As a thank you from us, you will receive 20% off every time a friend makes a first purchase. For full details on our Refer a Friend programme visit www.psbooks.co.uk/refer

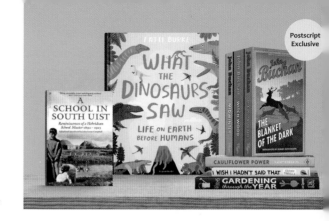

up to 75% off publishers' prices

Have you tried the Postscript website?

• Browse Postscript's full range of almost 10,000 discounted titles online at www.psbooks.co.uk

• Access exclusive offers, such as 3 for 2 promotions – only available online

• New titles and old favourites which have returned to stock are added regularly, giving online customers access to titles before they appear in a catalogue

• Our 'Recommended for you' function offers suggestions based on the genres, authors and publishers in your previous orders

• Almost Gone pages help ensure you don't miss out on titles that are in limited supply

Free UK delivery on orders over £25 online*

www.psbooks.co.uk
Order line: 01626 897100
(8am-6pm, Mon-Fri)

Postscript Books Ltd., 6 Battle Road, Heathfield, Newton Abbot, Devon TQ12 6RY

Our green packaging

Our commitment to sustainability includes how we produce our catalogues and despatch your books:

• Our catalogue is printed in the UK on paper from sustainably managed forests and is not shrink-wrapped; and many of our in-house Postscript Collections use simple paper bands rather than plastic wrapping

• All orders are despatched in recyclable cardboard boxes, eco-friendly bubblewrap and solvent-free labels, paper and tape

What our customers say

feefo ★★★★★

4.8/5 based on over 8,600 customer ratings

"Easy and quick transaction. Very satisfied buyer."
Firstly, I enjoyed reading their catalogue so that instead of buying one book for a present I bought another for myself. The books arrived very quickly and were well packaged. Ordering them was easy, a really uncomplicated transaction. Thank you.

"Excellent value"
Person on the phone was helpful and friendly. The order arrived within a few days. The books are such good value and my book club members always rate the books highly. Great value and postage is reasonable.

could not afford to keep him on. I got on well with Mr
Barnes and listened sympathetically to his complaints. He
had a Northern accent, and was slowly being driven out
of business by a grocer newly established in what is now
Bonn Square. 'It's them Grane Shaldes', he would say,
and in the end the Green Shields drove Mr Barnes out of
business, and he had to shut up shop.

Leaving the Green Shields area, one went, how sym-
bolically, downhill, into the square, passing the grim old
Salvation Army citadel with its tall brick tower – another
refuge for the poor and homeless. At night, you left behind
you the last street light and descended into the darkness
of the square. All lay silent there, the profound silence of
homesickness, of exile. In those days, there were no mug-
gers about, no drug-pushers; the poor endured their lot
with no expectation that life would or could be improved.

No, that was not entirely the case. There was crime
in the square. I decided I wanted to buy one of the old
houses on the other side of the square. Was it up for
£500? I really forget. But I had a dollar cheque from an
American magazine. I got to know the woman who lived
in that house, a pleasant enough person. Every morning,
she would step outside her front door and stare up to
her left, where Oxford Prison loomed over the square,
twinned with the Salvation Army citadel. Her husband
would wave to her from a barred prison window, and she
would wave back. It was but a step from one environment
to the other.

'He'll be out of there in another year,' she told me cheerfully. They planned to leave Oxford. I looked round her little house. The walls were paper thin, but I thought it might do for me and have a room for a study and typewriter. One peculiar feature was that the double bed in the front room overlooking the square was piled with fur coats. I did not understand or comment. While I was thinking over the prospect of buying the house, the police raided it. The stolen furs were retrieved, the woman was arrested, and the house was closed up.

There were other occupants where I lived in No. 12, each in his separate cell. Living at the top of the building was an eccentric undergraduate who collected rare old British army uniforms. He also drove a Land Rover, and was evidently a rung or two above the rest of us on the economic ladder. One day, when he was away, living with the Tuaregs, the ceiling of his room and part of the roof fell in. I rescued his precious army uniforms. On his return, he rewarded me with a gigantic brown teapot, before getting into his vehicle and driving back to Africa.

George Halcrow remained a good friend. When he came to collect the weekly rent, I was often hard pushed to find it. 'Oh well, never mind, Brian,' he would say. 'I'll try again next week.'

George had been the man who read people's gas meters. He fell in love with a penniless woman, the daughter of Edgar Wallace. Wallace had been immensely successful but had died in debt, spending his ample all on the racecourse. Shortly after daughter and gas man were married, German film-makers bought up all Wallace's short stories and made a grand succession of films from them. It was the luck of the draw for George. The happy pair were in the dibs. George could afford to forgo that 7s 6d; nevertheless, he did forgo it, as many in that situation would not have done. Good old George! For many a year, the German-made bust of Edgar Wallace could be seen in the bay window of George's house at No. 4 Bradmore Road: a present from the German film-makers.

I lived in my room for over a year. I had grown comfortable with the square and the back streets surrounding it. I slept on an army bed. My mother came to see me once, and brought me what I believe we used to call a counterpane. She was calm and sympathetic, perhaps clear in her belief that I would always end in a doss house.

She also brought Clive and Wendy to see where I lived. I thought poor Clive was shocked; putting his best face on it, knowing not what to say, he said, 'I like how clean it is, Daddy.' My dear, precious children . . .

A large cheque came from the States for my fiction – for *Hothouse*, as written by an exile looking back on India. I left the square before it was entirely closed down as I had enough cash to buy a little terraced house in Marston Street, where I finished writing *Greybeard*. The square's inhabitants were dispersed among various old folks' homes. Driving down the Botley Road, I often saw, coming from the new home on the right, people I knew – one old boy in particular, who had been permitted to keep his mongrel dog. He was often to be observed crossing the road to the tobacconist, with dog. I wondered if he had read George Orwell's *Down and Out in Paris and London*. Admittedly, the chances were fairly slim.

The community of the square was scattered – no longer could you buy a half of a quarter of butter anywhere, and the brutish multi-storey car park went up where No. 12 and the rest had stood. Lost were the old unity and an earlier age. Even the Salvation Army citadel went. The days of the supermarket and the credit card had arrived.

3

Hothouse

Hothouse

The old village street where I live now has few trees, although I have planted a copse in the further reaches of my garden. Trees, whether naked or clothed in leaves, depending on the season, are a source of pleasure, and often an exemplar of calm. The remorseless quality of trees is to be admired. How they survive despite urban crawl! Trees root themselves in the earth, as they have done since before intelligence tinkled its way into the world.

Supposing trees had taken up that intelligence, as animals have done? Then their roots might serve an additional purpose: to permit trees to move about, to escape the captivity of street ornamentation, to elude the perfectionist creators of bonsai, to attack the remorseless cutting down of woodlands, perhaps – if they perceived mankind as an enemy – even to advance upon railway tracks, upon motorways, upon grazing herds of sheep, even upon houses where the enemy lurks when not doing damage elsewhere.

Fortunately, that ability did not develop. The tree is helpless against the chainsaw. Yet it remains formidable.

I was once caught in a forest fire. There's nothing like a forest fire to teach you respect for trees. Particularly when the trees are battalions strong.

This occasion was staged in the final days of the Second World War, when the Japanese were ready to surrender their hold on the many countries of the Far East. Three of us, soldiers of the British Empire, formed a rearguard when the rest of the company had been flown out to the safety of Chittagong and India. We camped on the edge of a mighty forest, equipped with some drinking water but not provisions, awaiting a plane that would come and rescue us. That plane had already been delayed for a couple of days. The outbreak of peace was very disorganizing.

The situation in which we found ourselves was in the midst of two great stretches of forest, once one whole and undivided forest until someone, presumably the pre-war British who ruled Burma, had cut a great swath through the middle of it. That swath would have served as a landing strip for the biplanes then still privately in use. Given its neglect, that strip was now full of knee-high weeds, nothing more.

We awoke one morning to find the forest furiously on fire. The fire was then quite distant, but a stiff breeze blew the smoke towards us. The smoke and the fire! Soon it became evident that both sides of the strip were burning at the same rate, keeping pace with one another in military precision. This enormous, beautiful, terrifying conflagration, its flames blazing high above the highest branches, was rapidly approaching us and our bivouac. The growth on the strip itself burned out and blackened, always keeping pace with the main conflagration. How could we escape? Where should we go? If we ran, still the fire would overtake us. The sky itself seemed alight. The fire advanced remorselessly, leaving behind walls of blackened tree stumps.

My idea provided the one solution to our dilemma. I stepped out into the centre of the strip. My mates followed. The mighty conflagration roared down towards us. The weeds in the strip burned in sympathy. Noise and heat were overwhelming. Now the fire was at our sides, all-devouring. The weed growth, like an obedient lance corporal, kept pace, flaring briefly, leaving only ash behind its advance. The immense dual blaze was on us like a tiger, two tigers, with a great roar! We jumped. We jumped through that shallow rank of fire into the smouldering ash beyond. So we were safe, little more than scorched, and the great arboreal bonfire roared past us on either side.

Later, a jeep came, its driver surprised to find us still alive. It took us to a Dakota, a short distance away. The Dakota flew us over the mountains to a landing strip by Chittagong, then a stinking safe haven. The pilot, an American, regarded us in amazement. 'Did none of you guys throw up? If you were Americans you'd all have thrown up on that bumpy trip.' We explained to him that we had nothing to throw up with. We had been on, at best, half-rations for the previous six months.

India! We went to a rest camp at a place called Kanchrapara. From there we could catch a train into

Calcutta. In Calcutta, the cinemas were air-conditioned, and one could buy an OUP *Golden Treasury* bound in cardboard, and American SF magazines.

And one could cross the River Hooghly and again be among trees. This time, restful trees, well tended. And one particular tree. So, on a hot and golden day long ago, I hired a boatman to ferry me across the Hooghly to the Calcutta Botanical Gardens. There I spent an afternoon with friends, gazing at a famous Indian banyan tree. A notice proclaimed it to be the 'Biggest Tree in the World', not in height, like a sequoia, but in circumference. Great care was taken of this phenomenal tree. The banyan stretches out its branches horizontally; from these branches, roots extend downward into the ground, and so the tree creeps forward in all directions. It was old, and many branches were propped up by forked sticks, painted white to deter insects. The effect was as if Salvador Dalí had taken up arboriculture.

On my eventual return to England, I discovered that Julian Huxley, brother of Aldous Huxley, had written of this tree in an article, 'The Meaning of Death', in the *Cornhill*, a Victorian magazine and literary journal. That article appeared in the 1920s when, according to Huxley, the tree covered two acres. How many acres does it cover today, I wonder?

The England to which I returned in the fag-end of the 1940s was a grave disappointment. Whereas I had adjusted to the squalor and poverty of India, I hated the squalor and poverty, allied to a depressing climate, of my homeland. The rigours of the Second World War all but ruined Britain. The empire for which we had fought was no more. I had no connection. No money. I resolved to forget the East – 'the splendour and havoc of the East', as Alexander William Kinglake nobly calls it. There seemed no other way to come to terms with my new life.

Yet the outrageous subcontinent of India, the pagodas and the hardships of Burma, the broken-down beauty of Sumatra and its people, the cleanliness of Singapore, the swarming delights of Hong Kong, and all those rivers and warm seas in which my friends and I had swum – and that Dalí-like banyan – remained ineradicably in my mind. Naturally – for they had both made me and ruined me.

Exorcism was required. It was towards the end of 1959 that I wrote a short story called 'Hothouse' and sent it to the American *Magazine of Fantasy and Science Fiction*. There it was published in February 1961. It caught on, as they say. I had imagined a mango tree covering the world, encouraged by global warming, as the Sun began to go nova. The magazine editor kept asking me for more. So I was able to write of the adventurous journeys of Gren and his friends.

I was not particularly well acquainted with the tribal customs of science fiction readers. I had not heard of the Hugo Awards, the SF equivalent of an Oscar in the movie industry. However, one fine morning in 1962, my girlfriend went out to collect from her doorstep her pint of milk and found there a strange object wrapped in an Irish newspaper. When unwrapped, this proved to be a Hugo Award for 'Hothouse' and my short fiction. I gained the impression that possibly my luck was turning.

The complete *Hothouse* as you find it now was published in hardcover by Faber and Faber in 1962. That same year, Signet books (New American Library) also proposed publication; but the editor there said the manuscript was too long; they confined their books to 160 pages. So they proposed cutting out the section regarding the tummybelly men – the one humorous section of the novel. I wrote back, saying that if they removed my tummybelly men, then I would take the manuscript elsewhere.

Later, I was pleased I had stood my ground as a writer; and it remains a ground on which I have since often stood. Now well trampled, it fed me the confidence I had lacked. Signet graciously gave in. They kept the tummybelly men. I liked the tummybelly men; in other fictions, slaves who were liberated joined in the fight heartily on the side of their liberators. I could never believe that; my tummybelly men prove to be to their liberators nothing but a pain in the neck. Signet had their revenge. When I received my complimentary copies of the book I found it was entitled *The Long Afternoon of Earth*. I wrote to the editor, saying the title sounded more like Anthony Trollope than Brian Aldiss. Their rejoinder was pretty neat: 'Had we called it *Hothouse* the booksellers would have put it in the Gardening section.'

When I was adrift in Oxford in the 1960s I became friendly with C.S. Lewis. Well, perhaps it would be better to say that I was an acolyte, but we got together to found the Oxford Speculative Fiction Society. The term 'science fiction' was considered too plebeian. I gave CS a copy of *Hothouse* when it was published by Faber. He liked it enough to buy a copy to present to his friend J.R.R. Tolkien. Tolkien kindly wrote to me to say how much he enjoyed my novel. I was delighted. A month or two later a second letter arrived saying he had just reread *Hothouse* and liked it even more a second time.

Hothouse has gone through thirty or forty reprints and translations. This modest success comes perhaps because it is an account of a journey; a book on my shelves is *Travel Literature: The Evolution of the Novel* by Percy G. Adams, which title points convincingly to an order of precedence. Adams quotes from an essay by Levi-Strauss which offers some support for science fiction as an important literary form:

> that crucial moment in modern thought when, thanks to the great voyages of discovery, a human community which had believed itself to be complete and in its final form suddenly learned . . . that it was not alone, that it was part of a greater whole, and that, in order to achieve self-knowledge it must first of all contemplate its unrecognisable image in the mirror.

My compulsory 'voyage of discovery' in Burma, to India and elsewhere has left its permanent mark. The misfortune of a young man who returns to his native land after years away is that he finds that land foreign, whereas the foreign lands he has left behind, their dangers, their seductions, and their mango trees, remain forever like an enticing mirage in the mind. However, it is misfortune which helps fertilize the seeds of creativity.

And maybe the future will not lie in cities. Maybe people will wish to live buried up to their psyches in the countryside, having only electronic contact with other workers. The trees will grow round them, and tall grasses, and exotic plants, and folk will look about at landscape and the night sky and be the better for it. And maybe some of those creatures driven near extinction, the Bengal tiger for one, will silently return to tread, fly, or crawl in a land once solely theirs.

4

A Sight of Serbian Churches

A Sight of Serbian Churches

I once knew Slovenia well. When I first travelled here with my future wife, Margaret, in the 1960s it was one of the republics of President Tito's Yugoslavia. I had been reading the Victorian traveller, Alexander William Kinglake. At the beginning of *Eothen* (1844), he says, 'I had come to the end as it were of this wheel-going Europe, and now my eyes would see the splendour and havoc of the East.' This was the paragraph that set me to spend most of 1964 travelling round Yugoslavia in an old Land Rover with Margaret. Like Kinglake, I wrote only one travel book. Mine was *Cities and Stones: A Traveller's Jugoslavia* (1966). We also met with our share of splendour and havoc. That time has gone now. Margaret has gone. President Tito has gone. And Yugoslavia has gone with him.

To bone up for the trip I read Rebecca West's *Black Lamb and Grey Falcon* and, rather less heavy going, Ivo Andrić's *The Bridge Over the Drina*, in which the Serbs struggle against the Ottoman regime. Before leaving England, I visited the Yugoslav Embassy in London several times. I wished to make sure that our journeys would be welcome. There we were in the midst of the Cold War. The embassy proved wonderfully sombre. Communism brought muffled silences along with it. Heavy knap curtains were kept pulled over the long windows. I talked in the shadows to serious men who had shaved a week or so ago. One result of these visits was that we arranged we would drive, as soon as we crossed the frontier, to Belgrade. Travel in Yugoslavia in the 1960s was not easy; roads formed a vivid example of the advantage of staying put. But the country, for all its wild appearance, was remarkably safe, although few tourists made it to the interior.

In Belgrade we reported to Turisticki Savez, the Tourist Authority. They proved hospitable and gave us little glasses of vodka; it was the chill wintry day for which vodka had been designed. From a large safe, a woman official produced a greasy but official pile of petrol coupons for us. Armed with those coupons, we fortunately never had to pay for a single litre of Yugopetrol, not for all those thousands of kilometres we travelled.

Thanks to this generous advantage we spent very little. My publisher, Faber, had paid me a £70 advance for *Cities and Stones*; after half a year's travel, we returned to England with some of the advance unspent.

In a used Land Rover we toured all of Jugland (as we called it). We were wild and free. We lived like gypsies, sometimes sleeping in perfect safety on little greens in the middle of one town or another. Often we were soothed by a song popular at the time and sung with deep melancholy:

> Pod Moskovsky vec
> Pod Moskovsky vecera . . .

Oddly this same tune became popular in Britain too. 'Moscow nights' was played in a joyful swing version by Kenny Ball and his Jazzmen.

Every now and again we had to stay the night in a hotel to get a shower. Operating on Communist principles, staff of hotels were infallibly paid – probably enough to keep a slug alive. No incentive to improve existed. As a result, service was formidably slow. We developed the habit of saying, 'Prepencenica sljivovica, molim', as we entered the morgue-like dining rooms. To my mind, slivovitz, a kind of plum brandy, was one of the world's great alcoholic drinks – gone, alas, as has Yugoslavia itself.

No wonder Yugoslavia could not hold together: under the cloak of Communism were many conflicting religions and ideologies. Slovenia was mainly Catholic, Serbia was Orthodox, Croatia was Catholic, while Bosnia was predominently Muslim. Outside the fine city of Sarajevo lay Bogomil tombs; the Bogomils were a heretical sect believing in a kind of Manichaeism, a primitive belief in a conflict between God and the devil.

All these religions had their places of worship. Under Tito's mild version of Communism, the various religions lost something of their diversity. When Croatia celebrated Easter, no one seemed to mind. Many fine churches and mosques still survive. It says something for the Tito regime that these religions were not entirely suppressed. But the hostile attitude was clear when a scholarly Communist friend took us to inspect a fine church in Ljubljana. A service was in progress at the time, with prayers and hymns. This friend spoke loudly, strolling about as if the church were empty. I felt extremely bad; but it was a fine church and it was in operation, against all Communist contempt. Laid low by war and invasion, all these old churches were well looked after. In many places, restoration was still taking place – restoration of mosques as well as of Orthodox churches.

Time had taken its toll of much of the trove of art. Some destruction was deliberate. For this, the Turks took most of the blame. Yet Bulgarians, Russians, and others had often been responsible. Often the custodians were careless. In one church Margaret and I were investigating, the curator pulled open a table drawer and produced an illuminated document written on vellum. 'Have a look,' he said. 'It's the charter of the church.' I took the document he proffered. It was a fifteenth-century document – the only fifteenth-century document I have ever had in my hands. I was astounded. Surely this document should have been kept safely in a museum, in Belgrade or Ohrid. Even better, in the British Museum. Presumably the curator, as a good Communist, believed that everything belonged to the people – even to a benighted British tourist!

We visited a number of churches. The most beautiful churches, the most unworldly, were the Serbian monastery churches, many lost in the wilderness of the Sumadia. At about the time that Henry II was having trouble with Thomas à Beckett, the Nemanjič dynasty came to power in a state then called Rashka. This marked the beginning of what we know as the Serbian state. Many a fine church was built by the Nemanjičs, Hilander (Chilandari) on Mount Athos being one of them. Byzantium lasted for a thousand years, and the monastic churches of Serbia bear that lengthy Byzantine imprint. In the Serbian Orthodox churches, the light of Christianity found shelter during the dark centuries when the Balkans was submerged under Ottoman rule. Serbian landscapes – at least when I knew them in the 1960s – were placid and green, full of flowers, pigs, and cuckoos. Monastic churches were built here when the threat of the Turkish invader was real enough. Thus, many are hidden away, many are fortified. The contrast with English country churches, in the village, with the village pub nearby, is marked.

One such Serbian church is Manasija. Round Manasija was built a massive outer fortification, in which stand eleven square towers. When the building was finished in 1418, a garrison of soldiers was dispatched to defend the garrison of monks.

Inside, the church was darkly inspirational, inducing a state of reverence, even in an unbeliever. Walls and pillars were adorned with frescoes of saints, often warrior saints, and biblical pictures. There were no pews: an Orthodox believer stood before his Maker. Despite much damage over the centuries, the effect was one of mystery and grandeur, with gracious figures erect in lakes of blue and gold. Fresco colours were applied while the plaster was still wet; painting was a rapid business, avoiding some of the stiffness one sees in mosaics — as for instance in the splendid mosaics of Ravenna, far away.

But in Manasija no frescoes have survived below about shoulder height. This centre of reverence and learning was overwhelmed by the Ottomans, who stabled their horses in the church. Horses, traditionally blind to religion, rubbed their rear ends against the artwork. Their riders, the Ottomans, also tore lead and copper from the roof and from its five cupolas. Rain poured in, in equine indifference to the power and pictures of prayer.

So Manasija remained a ruin for centuries. The Communist government in Belgrade took it upon themselves to restore the church — despite almost the entire country's need to be rebuilt after the Nazi invasions of the Second World War. Why did they do that? Doubtless it was a matter of national pride, rather than religion. Many such churches are architectural masterpieces, too little known to the outside world.

Ravanica was also fortified. It had been restored by the 1960s, and a small guest house built within its walls. When we called, forty-two nuns lived there. They owned two tractors, some cows, and the ubiquitous black Serbian porker. They also had two peacocks, given to calling to each other in the middle of the night, and responding to train whistles by daylight – the railway line passed near by. Dogs in the nearby hills indulged in frenzies of barking. What with the vegetable strips and the simple sanitation, we felt ourselves back in medieval England. Our mood was entirely captured by the church. We felt compelled to linger there.

Margaret and I camped in the grounds of Ravanica. It poured with rain that night. The mother superior sent out to our tent some noodle soup to comfort us. The singing of the sisters in church was a delight, very touching, Christianity living under Communism. We remained for some days. We were in a trance, thinking we should never manage to return there. We never did. We never have.

Dečani! The most beautiful distant church; a century older than Magdalen College in Oxford. Dečani stands in the Kosmet – apparently it has survived the war that followed the collapse of Yugoslavia. While we were in Slovenia a summer past, I was happy to learn from friends that Dečani remains intact. The miseries of the Balkans when Slobodan Milosěvić was in power in Belgrade, together with the war in Kosovo, had no doubt threatened that glorious building.

I have never revisited Dečani. Like many a Serbian
church, it was not easy to get to. As I described it in *Cities
and Stones*, there were Albanian shepherd boys playing
their flutes on the mountains nearby, as others like them
must have done long ago, when this part of the world was
under the custody of Alexander of Macedon. The road
plunges down, past the patriarchate of Peč, and runs into
an afforested gorge. There we beheld this jewel, sunset
encouraging its marble facade to glow, sulphurous and
grand, in pink and yellow hues. Never has delicate beauty
so whispered of what is eternal.

We camped on a hillside where those ancient walls
could be glimpsed through the trees. The Nemanjičs – that
Serbian dynasty, strong in prayer and swordplay – were
responsible for the creation of Dečani, as for many of the
other Serbian churches we visited, the names of which
now form a magical roll call: Žiča, Ljubostinja, Studenica,
Manasija, Ravanica, Gracanica . . . . Stefan Uroš III inspired
the building of Dečani in 1327. It was completed by his
son, the great Dušan.

Dečani looked completely different from the monastery
at Peč, only ten miles away. Peč is Byzantine. Dečani,
however, was designed by a Catholic monk from Kotor,
Fra Vita, known as Vid, when the Nemanjičs were flirting
with Rome.

We were allowed inside this august monument, and
taken to an upper room, where the brothers gave me the
traditional *slatko*, to be washed down with the *vin rosé* of

Dečani. On the wall were photographs of President Tito at Dečani, flanked by metropolitans of the Serbian Orthodox Church. We conversed, I in my limited Serbian. I wanted food for Margaret, who had been taken ill.

Peace and goodwill filled the great spidery grey room, but the monks had not even an egg to spare. Eight of them only remained, gentle fellows, showing little of a religious spirit. They lived parsimoniously, on bread, milk products such as cheese, eggs, and honey. They invited me to stay with them for a month; but Margaret could not be housed, since she was a woman. My concern for her seemed to provoke their curiosity.

In the local sad little village, Dečani, no one had eggs to sell. I bought some canned grapes. When opened, the can proved to be half full of juice. It was a reminder of the scarcities under which people of the Balkans had lived for many centuries. I felt a certain envy; the true religious spirit is frequently a close neighbour to poverty. Accustomed though we were to frugal rations, it was hunger that drove us away from the area. But I had taken an opportunity to gaze at the thousand various paintings contained inside holy Dečani. These the great Dušan had commissioned after his father's death. There were portraits of Dušan himself here, and of all the Nemanjičs, together with portraits of the saints and illustrations from the New Testament. There were also 365 separate paintings for every day of the year. The first congregations would have been illiterate: here was their Bible, the gospels made flesh – or marble at least.

Dušan promulgated an important legal code, the Zakonik, to strengthen the organization of his empire – which would never be as strong or extensive again. He planned to rule as emperor from Constantinople, bringing new life into its withered courts. He died in his prime in 1355, some say on the march to Constantinople.

Very shortly after Dušan's burial, five centuries of Turkish rule closed like a shutter over the Balkans. Somehow, beautiful Dečani survives amid its orchards, as it survived the recent wars. Maybe it was its beauty as well as its sanctity which protected it. However, since the old Turkish bridge over the blue-eyed River Neretva in Mostar was destroyed in the fighting, we might conclude that luck, simple good luck, played a part in Dečani's preservation.

In an Orthodox church service, the congregation stands. There are no hymns, there is no instrumental music. The singers who chant the offices stand among the rest of the congregation. There is no surpliced choir as in our churches. Voices reverberate within the church, magnified by the acoustic properties of the dome.

Inside the little white church of Studenica, the con-gregation assembled among an extraordinary range of murals. These murals depicted the life of the Virgin Mary, from her birth to her death. Here we saw St Anna, Mary's mother, as well as a little curly-haired boy Jesus. It was a startling array of events, boldly drawn. The people here, dressed in softly flowing robes, were mainly youthful.

44

Young girls walked softly, spoke in whispers, smiled. Yet in the depiction of the death of the Virgin, there were genuine and moving representations of grief. A woman with her head lowered covered her mouth, while tears welled from her eyes. The Serbs were taught to be strong on sorrow. We also saw everyday things. Young goats attacking trees, lambs skipping, a boy about to feed a donkey.

Here was displayed part of the great medieval heritage of Serbian art, which has miraculously survived to the present day. True, time and desecration have taken place; nevertheless, much has been retrieved and preserved.

We were glad to be able to buy a series of small booklets, published in Belgrade early in the 1960s, each dealing with a separate church. Too often, we were hustled on by our guides, blind to both religion and art, after hours of travel to reach our destination. The booklets enabled us to study details of the wall paintings at leisure.

But we seized the opportunity to gaze on the portrait of King Milutin, founder of the church of Studenica. He held in his delicate hands, as he scowled majestically ahead, a model of the church, the King's Church. Next to him stood his child-wife, Simonis, daughter of a Byzantine emperor. Unlike the simply clothed holy figures of the other murals, both Milutin and his queen were richly robed, their clothes studded with jewels. Despite his four tumultuous marriages, Milutin wore a halo.

Talking about these remarkable Serbian churches, I emphasized the difficulty of getting to them. However, this was not the case with the monastic church of Žiča (pronounced Zheecha). Žiča was built before the Balkans had felt the blade of the sultan's sword, when there was no need for concealment; one could see it from some kilometres distant, standing out across the plain. This visibility of the monastery did not serve it well. The frescoes destroyed by Austrians in the First World War were restored in time to be destroyed by the Nazi forces in the Second. It was left to the Yugoslav Communists to perform a complete restoration in the 1950s and 1960s.

So there Žiča stood, brick-built, a landmark in landscape and Serbian history, proud and rose red, the colour of royalty: but in early dawn light the harsh tones became powdered roses, beautiful and to be wondered at. King Stefan Prvovenčani, the second son of Zupan Stefan, founded Žiča in the thirteenth century, building it on the frontiers of his territory about the time that King John in England was writing the Magna Carta. Stefan was the first Nemanja to wear the crown of Serbia. After him, six more kings were crowned in Žiča, and for each of them a new door was opened up in the red walls. On a screen, executed only in 1937, were portraits of these seven kings, each holding up for admiration the churches they founded. Formidable old men they looked, bearded and berobed.

The lands and properties of Žiča were largely confiscated by the Communist regime. A few acres alone remain, including a marsh full of loquacious frogs. Yet ancient traditions of hospitality were not entirely lost. We were given permission to camp within the monastic walls, close to the monastery itself – or, rather, nunnery in these days. We were invited indoors. Three sisters knelt in prayer, illuminated by a single candle, images of an ancient holiness. We entered a kitchen. It resembled a spartan early Victorian kitchen, with heavy furniture and evidence of much scrubbing of tables and floor. An ancient monk sat in a chair by an empty grate; he greeted us courteously.

We ate supper at table with the sisters. After a bowl of nettle soup accompanied by bread came poached eggs and bread. We drank water – which we feared had come from the marsh where the frogs held forth. No slivovitz here! The meal was taken in absolute silence, while a monk perched in an alcove read from holy scriptures, to guarantee that the soul was fed as well as – or better than – the stomach.

Enclosed in Žiča's grounds was a small church of more recent date than the main building. Here we found a portrait of Tzar Nicholas, looking remarkably like his cousin, George V of Britain. The Russian ruling house took an interest in the Serbian Orthodox churches, and particularly in Žiča. But the Russian artists employed here in the days of Joe Stalin were funded by a woman in Belgrade. Our guides told us that her son had died. In her grief, she had the small church built and decorated in his honour; she then became a nun herself. We were also told that a golden thread ('Žiča' means 'golden thread') had led Stefan Prvovenčani to this site. Our Communist interpreters related these sentimental tales, adding their chilly rational comments afterwards.

Margaret and I slept well in our little tent. We were roused early in the morning by the tolling of a bell in the wooden belfry. Down in the marsh, the frogs were tuning up for the day. We made our frugal breakfast of camomile tea and bread and butter, and packed our things into the Land Rover. When the old monk came to open the great wooden outer gates, we were in good spirits, ready to roll away from rose-red Žiča. Next, we planned to visit Ljubostinja down what passed, in those distant days, for a pretty good road.

When you reach the monastic church of Ljubostinja in deepest Serbia, you return to the nineteenth century. Of course, I am talking about the visit Margaret and I made; the present day may have crept up on Ljubostinja, in the fashion of all present days. In those distant times, the nuns welcomed you and showed you round. Yet there was a feeling that they were keen to get back to resume a leisurely lunch. Religion was a matter of private convenience which could be postponed until after tea. Perhaps prayer became more convincing when the shades of night had fallen. The nuns said that in winter their beautiful church was so cold they preferred to hold services in their cosier house. It was a pretty house. Lemon trees stood primly in tubs on its steps.

They bore fruit as early as May; a striking example of prayer bringing on vegetables.

The interior of Ljubostinja's church, built in the Morava style of architecture, was calm and sweet. Among the few surviving frescoes were portraits of Prince Lazar and his wife, the Princess Milica. Lazar died in battle – the notorious battle of Kosovo in 1389, against the forces of Sultan Murat II. Lazar's widow founded the monastery, to retire there under the name of Sister Eugenia. Other widows of Serbian nobles joined her. From this sad aspect of Serbian history, a feminine aura has been distilled.

The nuns had a house they devoted to handicrafts in the grounds. Earning a few extra dinars was evidently a necessity. Margaret got excited and bought several of their baskets, some of which, half a century later, still hold together. Although weaving and worship were pre-eminent in Ljubostinja, there was also a farm where hens pecked at the very steps of the church. A belfry, wells containing good water, and carefully planted trees, all added to a placid atmosphere that suggested an effective pattern of peace on earth. Among the many women who found refuge in Ljubostinja was Jelenia who, as Sister Jefimija, became the first Serbian woman of letters. Some of her illuminated work could be inspected in the church.

Also in the church, concealed under a carpet, lay Prince Lazar's Serbian eagle. For four hundred years, during the reign of the Turk, the eagle was lost in the woods: much as the little republics of former Yugoslavia were lost to the world at large. Margaret and I were among the early Westerners to visit these beautiful and curious havens. We felt at Ljubostinja that the nuns, polite as they were, did not wish us to hang about.

We would have stayed. We would have fasted, as we already had. We would have attended their religious services. But the nuns had their own lives, their own routines. That we perfectly understood; but it was with regret we climbed back into our Land Rover and drove away . . . to see the great wooden gates close promptly behind us. In those days, memories of the partisan resistance to invading German armies were deliberately kept fresh.

Near Ravanica stood the village of Senje. We were deep in Serbia, deep in the Balkans, no great distance from the Romanian and Bulgarian borders. Perhaps because I was reading Dostoevsky's *House of the Dead* at the time, I felt Senje might have been in Russia. Its long wandering road was fringed by ragged-elbow houses, all patched and worn and worried. The railway depot formed a centre for convivial life – if conviviality is the word I'm looking for. There a drink shop sinking in grime sold beer and slivovitz. From misty tumblers, the fierce liquid was poured down unshaven throats as if to quench internal fires.

The road was a river of mud in winter, a feather bed of dust in summer. We encountered a wedding procession. Behind the more-or-less happy couple lumbered an ox cart, laden with wedding gifts: beautiful sheets, blankets, spotless pillows, dresses decked with fine embroidery, all arranged to display themselves to the onlookers. A cart full of furniture was also doing the tour, exhibiting everything to the villagers. A large slippery wardrobe perpetually threatened to slide off the cart to the ground and had to be shoved back by willing guests.

Later, the guests began to dance. An accordion and a flute encouraged them. Margaret and I sat in the sun outside a little gostilna, eating cold palachinke (pancakes) with marmalade, wishing we might join in. The guests got in a muddle. They tried to dance the traditional kolo, but had forgotten how. Their celebrations were rather muted in consequence. We were witnessing the passing of an old order. Probably several old orders.

A threat to the peace of Ravanica were the buses which rolled in on a Sunday from Nicš or Svetozarevo (now Jagodina), to disgorge youths armed with footballs or guitars outside the monastery. One attraction was the caves behind the monastery, where a system of natural tunnels led one into the mountains. We ventured in a kilometre or more, to be stopped by a rushing water course. As we emerged into daylight again, school children rather sweetly greeted us with bunches of lilac, calling us 'The Kon-Tiki Expedition'.

At night, we heard wolves howling in the mountains as if to awaken the Nemanjičs from their long sleep.

The sisters of Ravanica were more hospitable than the nuns of Ljubostinja. We found them kind and delicate.

They welcomed us with the traditional *slatko*, which took the form of honey and water. We supped and talked to them while bees buzzed overhead in the horse chestnut trees. One asked us about that distant land from whence we came – England. We were able to buy eggs and brown bread from them. They apologized for the bread, saying brown bread was intended only for peasants, but it tasted good. We attended their services. So did a number of old women from Senje, all clad in black. One of them was crippled with rheumatism and could not kneel on the floor. A friend supported her. The sisters dressed modestly in sombre black, but two priests who conducted the service were splendidly arrayed in colourful gowns. Their long hair and beards were combed and oiled. The younger of the two kept fiddling with and primping his hair.

The singing of the sisters went straight to the heart. Their voices merged in a strange note of longing and regret. One catches that note also in ordinary Serbian love songs. Possibly it carries an intonation from the East, from India, transmitted through the courts of Byzantium. Their hymns, whether solo or in unison or descant, were moving and disturbing. They lingered in the mind long after the music had ceased.

I heard that same singing in the central church of Macedonia, which borders on Serbia, when I visited in 2001. The church stands in Veles and it is claimed to be the oldest church in Macedonia – now a land-locked state in its own right, and a land of beautiful countryside. The population is too sparse to domesticate it.

One Sunday, two friends of mine, Zlatko and Ljupco, escorted us up a cobbled hill path to the impressive church. From the square outside the church there were beautiful views to be seen. One looks across a valley where the River Vardar flows, rolling grandly between distant hills as yet unspoilt by the motorways of modern wheel-going Europe.

My friends knew the priest. He was a genial man who, when we appeared, was sitting in an ill-lit wood-panelled room, tapping away on his computer. He had just baptized a child; a deaconess was throwing away the bowl of holy water on a flower bed outside the church. An old man sat in a corner of the room, shrouding himself in cigarette smoke without speaking.

The priest readily gave us a tour of the church. It proved to be a large and complex building. As a rare privilege, we were conducted behind the iconostasis. After putting away the communion equipment, the priest flung himself into a fit of kissing everything in sight. Everything got kissed. We stood back. He exhibited to us his various robes, lifting them carefully from a wardrobe. Each was designed for particular ecclesiastical occasions. On many of them, the priest's portrait had been sewn. Egotism, I judged, rather than reverence.

The grand old church itself was fairly decrepit. The roof leaked, they said. We climbed a creaking stairway, to gain a balcony high above the tiled floor below. From there, we watched a wedding ceremony in progress. Smartly dressed guests clustered between tall candles. An elderly priest held crowns above the heads of bride and bridegroom.

Ljupco talked about the parlous state of the edifice. Macedonia was a small country, with a population of about 2 million. It was hard to raise the money needed for restoration. As we were leaving, we came on a collection box by the doorway. I brought out a $20 bill from my pocket and was about to stuff it into the box when Zlatko grasped my wrist. 'You are kind,' he said, 'but you are not a believer. We must raise the money ourselves.' I was impressed, and used the incident in my novel, *Affairs at Hampden Ferrers* (2004).

We emerged into the sunshine as the wedding party appeared in the square while, coming from another door, several people were holding hands, girls were skipping, everyone was smiling. They disappeared round a corner of Sveti Pantilimon. Another party of a different kind appeared from the opposite direction. They began slowly to cross the square towards the door through which the wedding party had just left. They consisted in part of three men and a woman, all dressed in black. Two of the men carried a stretcher between them. On the stretcher, covered by a cloth, lay a corpse. They crossed the square and entered into the church with their burden. We had witnessed the role a church plays in the life of the people

– in particular, in important moments of life, a baptism, a marriage, a death. Zlatko and I fell silent.

I conclude this account by saying that Yugoslavia – Jugland, as we always affectionately call it – has played a role in all our family's lives. My daughter Wendy, when quite a young girl, visited Ljubljana, where a friend, Vesna, and her family took Wendy to the islands of the Adriatic. We are still in touch with Vesna, and with her husband and children.

I collected several LP records of Jug music to which my children when young liked to dance. All have visited and holidayed in various parts. In 2006 my book *Cities and Stones* was translated into Croat and published in Zagreb. I went over for the launch. 'Why are you doing this?' I asked my publisher in amazement. 'It's an old book!' 'It is history,' he said. The Communists have gone. The churches remain.

Yugoslavia is no more. But we all benefited from it and have never forgotten that remarkable country. And the faith we found there, besieged? In the West we have largely lost faith. We are too wealthy, perhaps too enlightened. But it is impossible to look back on those little – and little known – churches without something like regret.

5

zulu

Zulu

And a Film That Never Was

As one who labours and dreams in solitude, I am always interested in the way creative people work together, submitting their egos to a community – often a community of varied talents and opinions. To get the work done, conflicting personalities must contribute towards what they – and we – trust will be a viable and profitable conclusion. This is how the art of the cinema functions.

Sometimes the conflict of many interests must seem almost irreconcilable. The fruits of cooperation between two major oppositions can be clearly seen in that remarkable film, *Zulu* (1964), where white and black actors collaborate. In these days of political correctness, the spectacle of white soldiers fighting black warriors might seem, to the stiff-necked, improper. However, not colour but courage is the theme of this masterly work. The storyline is simple in essence. It acquires mythic status. The year is 1879. Rorke's Drift is a small outpost, manned by a contingent of a Welsh regiment. It is attacked by warriors who greatly outnumber the soldiery in the post. They are repelled. And that's it.

Zulu was funded by Joseph E. Levine, who showed considerable faith in the newly founded Diamond Films company. Diamond was headed by Cy Endfield and Stanley Baker, both of whom overcame great difficulties to make the film, which was developed from an article by John Prebble.

In Natal, Endfield and Baker formed a friendship with Zulu Chief Buthelezi. Buthelezi spoke English and had soldiered in Sandhurst. He was keen to engage his men to act in the great slaughter depicted in the battle of a little missionary station known as Rorke's Drift, Natal.

The Zulus had never seen a camera before. Comedy films were ordered up from South Africa. A large stone was painted white to serve as screen, on which were projected such early comedies as Harold Lloyd, Laurel and Hardy, and Buster Keaton. The audience was enchanted. They fell on their backs laughing. From then on they 'wanted to be in the movies', and gladly took direction in the making of the film. Great friendships were forged and, at least until recently, an annual celebration was held by black and white actors together, celebrating the commencement of shooting. The scenes in the burning hospital were shot later at Pinewood; otherwise, everything was filmed in Natal. Those august mountainsides, those prodigious dawns, are all authentic: and come to us, accompanied by the exhilarating music of John Barry, as fresh today as when the film was first released in 1963. Barry's score contributes greatly to the success of the movie and seemed to speak thunderously of battle and courage.

Cy Endfield as producer/director and Stanley Baker as producer/star have shown what amounts to genius in the staging of this story, which achieves a fine tragic quality. There is no triumphalism when the Zulus finally call off their attacks; only a roll call of the missing troops, only the fatigue and sickness of the two rival lieutenants. There are no heroics, no mawkishness, if we exclude one soldier's affection for a dying calf. Otherwise, the actors are beyond praise. Nigel Green is the deep-voiced, be-whiskered, unflappable, colour sergeant. Patrick Magee plays the savage surgeon major, up to his elbows in blood. Hookie, the bumptious, malingering old sweat, is unforgettably played by James Booth. Jack Hawkins has the rather irritating role of the Revd Witt, a secret drinker. Ulla Jacobsson plays Witt's dainty daughter, Margaret. Chief Cetewayo lets them leave; Lieutenant Chard orders them to leave.

Much of the drama is carried by the two leading actors. Michael Caine plays the role, unusual for him, of the dandyish Captain Bromhead, descendant of more than one generation of high-ranking officers. Opposing him is Chard, a captain of engineers, in Natal to build a bridge; ultimately, it is he, played by Stanley Baker, who takes command of the small besieged force. These two execute a masque of conflict and eventual collaboration. But the bickering between the two officers, though important in its outcome, is petty in comparison with the oncoming threat of attack on Rorke's Drift. The uneasy relationship between the two officers acts as a vivid foil against the major task of fending off assailing Zulus, who attack in their hundreds.

The film opens just after the massacre at Isandhlwana. At Isandhlwana, Zulu warriors slaughtered twelve hundred British soldiers. We see the victors tramping among the dead, collecting up rifles they will use later against the defenders of the missionary station. A mass marriage takes place, warriors dancing to a row of bare-breasted young women. It is here that the Revd Witt learns of the slaughter at Isandhlwana, and hastens to give Rorke's Drift news of their impending slaughter.

The scene where the Gallopers are passing by the Drift, not stopping, not helping in the defence, is striking. Chard tries to stop them. 'We need you!' But the horsemen gallop onwards, hardly pausing in their retreat. Chard turns angrily to Bromhead. 'You knew them. Why did you not speak up?' To which Bromhead responds, 'You're in charge here now, old boy.' Everyone in the Drift stands staring appalled as the mounted men disappear into the distance.

The soldiery is stricken and silent. That is, until the colour sergeant says, 'All right, no one told you to stop work.' So the business of building defences continues. A young soldier, in fear and trembling, asks the colour sergeant, 'Why does it have to be us, sar'nt?' To which the deep and steady voice replies, 'Because we're 'ere, lad.'

So much for the military actors. The Zulus have no speaking parts – which is not to claim they do not sing. They are a force of nature; they are born of this harsh country. It's their country. The first indication of their coming, before we see them, is the continuous rattling of their spears on shields – an early form of psychological warfare. Bromhead asks in a puzzled way if this is the sound of a train. He soon learns the truth of it. On the brows of neighbouring hills, the Zulu force appears.

Hundreds of them are ranged there, chanting their deep-throated battle cry. Surely they are simply too many for any regiment to stand against. And some of course are armed with the rifles acquired at Isandhlwana. The military detachment has no alternative but to stand and fight.

On the Zulus come, in the first of many assaults. The thin red line opens fire. Exhausted though the soldiers become, they never give up. Even the sick in hospital, such as Hookie, stand against the continual waves of fearless Zulus.

No doubt this is a 'man's film'. The defenders ward off the attackers, not without their own losses but with dead bodies piling up beyond the hastily erected ramparts. There is no glorying in this result, hardly even a sense of victory. Bromhead and Chard each wearily express their disgust at the carnage. Standing amid the smouldering remains of the hospital, Chard says, 'I came here to build a bridge.' Bromhead admits, 'I feel sick.'

To close, no flag-waving. The colour sergeant reads the roll call; many names are missing. Then the voice-over tells us that eleven Victoria Crosses were awarded for bravery in the battle of Rorke's Drift. We see these exhausted heroes one by one. This understatement of victory, unusual in itself, projects no great demonstration of British armed power, but of dignity, of regret that it all had to happen, that the brave met the brave, with the retiring defeated force hailing the Drift survivors as fellow braves. These emphases alone are enough to make the film stand apart from almost all other battle movies.

I have said enough to indicate the movie's unique quality, yet not quite enough. Behind the scenes was another struggle. Cy Endfield was an American film-maker, forced to leave the USA during Joe McCarthy's anti-communist witch hunt. Finance for *Zulu* came from the American movie mogul Joseph E. Levine. Also, the Zulus, who act with such enthusiasm, applaud a British feat of arms. A monument to British fortitude, it owes much to America.

To this, a postscript must be added. Like so many Americans with technical competence, Cy Endfield read a lot of science fiction, particularly enjoying my novel, *Hothouse*. He approached me with an idea for an SF movie to be called *Only Tomorrow*, and asked me to collaborate with him. I was content to fry my own fish, and told Cy I did not want to do it.

At a London conference, I was up on the podium, in the middle of a speech. It was a vast room, full of people. At the far end of this chamber were continental-style double doors. They were flung open and a chubby man entered, holding a cablegram above his head. It was Cy. He had just received word from Joe Levine that Joe would fund *Only Tomorrow* to the extent of – what was the figure? – possibly 3 million dollars.

'*Now* will you join me?' asked Cy. I did so. Money does tend to induce realism – not to mention fantasy – into one's life. I was at once engaged in a preposterous plot in which alien human-look-alikes have a base on the dark side of the Moon, while planning to invade Earth.

Cy and his wife lived in Thurloe Square in London. He liked me to work there. He was so full of ideas that progress was difficult. First of all, the aliens had secret offices on Earth, which could be entered only through a seedy Chinese restaurant in England. Then, no, on the contrary, they had offices in LA with vast glass frontages. And Cy had discovered you could rent the Golden Gate Bridge for an hour, at a reasonable price.

We were still working on this plot when Cy's next film, following *Zulu*, became ready for showing. This was in 1965. A special first screening was arranged in a cosy little private cinema in the West End. I was invited, with my wife Margaret, together with many eminent names in the movie world, including a senior executive in the Levine organization. The film was entitled *Sands of the Kalahari*: another African setting.

A charter plane is forced down in the desert by a plague of locusts, and the passengers proceed to be nasty to one another. Stanley Baker has to wrestle with a baboon. The sands of the Kalahari are overrun with the dangerous beasts.

The film ended. The little cinema contained a chill silence. The representative of the Levine organization was first to leave, closely followed by a tinkle of ice cubes.

The offer of funding for *Only Tomorrow* was withdrawn. Cy went to Spain to make a different film.

What is beyond understanding is how Cy seemed not to know the difference between the stature of *Zulu* and the wastes of tosh. Although it is equally true that a writer never quite knows why one of his novels is taken up while another is passed over in silence. The tinkle of ice cubes remains an ever-present background theme.

Cy and I liked each other. I sympathized with his misfortunes. His film *Only Tomorrow* was never made. And soon Stanley Kubrick's magnificent movie *2001: A Space Odyssey* was filling the cinemas, a revelation of how a science fiction film can be an art form – much as *Zulu* shows how carnage can be an art form. No wonder either art form appears so rarely.

One can write a novel for free. One cannot make a movie for free. Scriptwriters often have to sacrifice creativity for the greater good: continuing finance. Three films have emerged from my novels, and I have seen this pressure at work.

Roger Corman was a delightful man, a calm director, and the theme of money wafts gently over the title of his autobiography, *How I Made a Hundred Movies in Hollywood and Never Lost a Dime*. He never lost a dime on the film he made from my novel *Frankenstein Unbound*, and indeed was so generous that he invited me and my family to stay in a hotel on the edge of Lake Como in Italy to see him shoot the movie, with John Hurt in the major role. The role of Percy Shelley was played by a pop star, Michael Hutchence. Hutchence was intelligent and had read up about Shelley; my younger daughter immediately fell in love with him. This is a film with a pleasant background.

Corman was friendly, and I persuaded him and his wife, Julie, to come and be stars at the Confluence of the Fantastic in the Arts (ICFA), which I attended in Florida every year. Both of them were deservedly popular.

I have written elsewhere how I came to write the touching little story 'Super-Toys Last All Summer Long' – a gentle, rather poetic title, not without a hint of disquiet; we all know summers do not last. Stanley Kubrick bought the story after painful negotiations, and I went to work with him on a screenplay. He wished to make a modern Pinocchio, whereas I hoped for something less backward-looking. Eventually, he kicked me out. Two other writers came and went. My belief is that Stanley was becoming unwell: he died before the film was half-made.

If the title meant anything, it implied that the script-writer should have had a poetic sensibility. As it is, the resultant script has a muddle of inconsistencies. We are given to understand that David, the android boy, disin-tegrates if something goes down his throat. Yet when immersed in water in a swimming pool he comes to no harm. So then later he determines to commit suicide by jumping into the river.

This is sad work, but Kubrick's friend Steven Spielberg was already at work completing the movie. Rereading the first little story, I saw how it all might end, and wrote to Steven to that effect. He wrote back, offering me a generous sum of money for one sentence in my letter. An honest dealer! I then wrote out an end story, taking care to include exactly the sentence I was paid for. So *A.I.* appeared in 2001, 'for Stanley Kubrick', and was quite a success.

A strange business, film-making, but I can boast that I have sold material to both Stanley Kubrick and Steven Spielberg, two of the great film-makers of the age.

6

The Ashgabat Trip

The Ashgabat Trip

Somewhere East of Life is one of my favourite books – a silly thing to say, but I like its way of slinking across genre barriers, of linking past, present, and future. My central character, Burnell, was forced to visit Ashgabat, the capital of Turkmenistan. During my research, I came across the name of a literary newspaper, published in Ashgabat, and wrote to the editor asking him if he could tell me what the state of religion was in his country. No answer. Meanwhile, Burnell was obliged to lecture at short notice at Ashgabat University. (Was there such an institution? I was guessing.)

I was doing what might grandly be called research for a novel which would cover some of the problems of the contemporary world. Turkmenistan held a particular attraction for me, not least because it is so little written about, so little visited. The country is the size of France, and most of it consists of the forbidding Kara Kum desert.

Some while after Malcolm Edwards, my editor at HarperCollins, had accepted my novel, I received a letter from Mr Tirkish whose address in Ashgabat I had managed to discover. I had not realized that mail still travels via

71

Moscow, and Moscow was in no great hurry to forward the mail. Anyhow, what Mr Tirkish wrote made good sense. He said that the religious situation was too complex for explanation in a letter; I was welcome to visit him in Ashgabat where he and his son would entertain me.

'Ashgabat? Where's that?' I've heard the question many times.

With the collapse of the Soviet Union, new nations came into being. In place of what had been marked Soviet Central Asia on the map stood five newly independent states, Kazakhstan, Uzbekistan, Turkmenistan, Tajikistan, and Kirghizia (now Kyrgyzstan). The mere names awaken curiosity. The republics stretch from the Caspian Sea to the frontiers with China, and are home to about 50 million people. Of these populations, only about 4 million live in Turkmenistan.

Turkmenistan is the most westerly republic and Ashgabat is its capital. It borders the Caspian Sea, and has for its southern neighbours Iran and Afghanistan. It is not easy to get to Ashgabat. You can fly via Moscow or via Istanbul. Flying time is something like eight hours.

Meanwhile, Mr Tirkish gave me the name and phone number of a Turkmen living in Reading which has a small Turkmen community. I phoned Dr Yousef Azemoun, who had been Minister for Culture in Turkmenistan, who said that by chance he and his wife, Guzin, were going to hold a festivity the next week. Would I like to come along?

'Should I get involved?' I asked Margaret. 'You are already involved,' she replied.

Both Yousef and Guzin were extremely hospitable. Guzin cooked like a dream, a dream of mysterious foodstuffs of wondrous flavours. Yousef was a man of great charm and intellect. From that string of new republics hanging together like washing on the line from the Caspian to the frontiers of China came many fugitives to the party, jolly men and women, glad to join in. Although they were Muslim, seventy years of Russian domination had taught them to drink vodka like Russians.

I spent a number of happy evenings with Yousef and Guzin, and one day Yousef announced that he was going to visit Ashgabat and would I like to go with him?

Ashgabat! 'A short coach ride to nowhere', said the guidebook. Actually, it is quite an amazing city, all rebuilt after a devastating earthquake in 1948. In many of the central streets, little gullies beside the pavements bear running water in order to cool the temperature. The city could teach Headington in Oxford a thing or two, being clean and well swept.

On the city's edge were barriers – not to keep citizens in but to keep camels out. The camels, slobbering in the extremes of dejection, stood behind the bar awaiting water or unemployment pay, neither of which were forthcoming. The desert lies in wait beyond the city borders. It's a miracle of human endeavour that the place exists at all. I found it a peaceful place, slowly waking up. There were no guns there and no pollution.

The President of Turkmenistan was one Saparamurat Niyazov, a sturdy man with a crop of bright yellow dyed hair. He is dead now. He was mocked in the West but was popular with his people, although a notorious joke in Turkmenistan concerns him. Instead of improving the ruinous infrastructure of his domain, Niyazov had a gold statue of himself erected in the public square, which slowly revolved so that it always faced the sun. So the joke goes that he and his wife went out onto the bedroom balcony of their palace and were greeted by the newly risen sun:

'Oh great Niyazov, greatest of the great, I, your willing slave, greet you.' At noon Niyazov again went onto his balcony. 'Oh great Lord, grandest of the grand above all, how gladly I, your willing slave, greet you once more.' So in the evening, when the sun was low, Niyazov went again to his balcony. This time the sun had nothing to say. 'Well, sun, have you no praise to give me?' And the sun replied, 'Get lost, you old poofter! I'm safe in the West now.'

When I arrived with Yousef it was Makhtumkuli Day. Makhtumkuli was an eighteenth-century Sufi poet, who has also become subject to a cult of personality. His gloomy statues fill the parks. In a quest for national identity, these rather remote Asian republics adopt national heroes. In some regions, Genghis Khan is back in favour. But in Turkmenistan, the elite – to wit, President Saparmurat Niyazov – had chosen a poet, Makhtumkuli. It's as though we had Shakespeare or Marlowe atop Nelson's Column instead of the Admiral.

74

A ceremonial yurt had been erected in the main square. Niyazov stepped out of a sedan car. There was no motorcade. He had no escort of motorcyclists; nor were there armed men on every rooftop. He walked among the crowds. I stood six feet from him and photographed him and his funny hair. No one snatched the camera from me. He disappeared into the yurt.

The strange ruler had been low man on the Soviet totem pole. But when the Communists faded away like the smile on the face of the Cheshire cat, there he was, in emulation of Lord Byron who awoke one morning and found himself famous, so Niyazov awoke and found he was in charge of a whole country. He rechristened the KGB the Popular People's Party and things went on much as they had done before.

Yousef had with him a journalist, a witty young woman called Sue Waldram, from the BBC. We were installed in a hotel we knew as the Nadir. I had a radio which could be tuned to two stations only, both of them Radio Moscow One. I had a fridge in which I kept some bars of German chocolate and a bottle of mineral water – together with dozens of baby cockroaches.

One morning I awoke early. The sun was already up in a cloudless sky. Cuckoos were cuckooing, a heart-crushing English-type song. I fancied a stroll along the sunlit empty streets. As I went down the bare concrete steps to the ground floor, I encountered a woman cleaning. She was glad to see a living human. She set down her broom and then addressed me, with gestures, in the only words of English she knew: 'The day. The street. The trees. The sky. The sun.' She swept her arm above her head as if to encompass all the lovely things of which she spoke. No rhetoric could have been more moving.

I followed in the phantom footsteps of my character, Burnell. Burnell is invited at short notice to lecture at Ashgabat University. ('I suppose there must be a university,' I had said to myself.) It was rather creepy to find it existed – and that I too was invited to lecture there at short notice. I said yes. I went to the university and addressed a senior class. They were so bright that for once I could dispense with an interpreter. They burned with curiosity about the outside world from which they were debarred. My reception was much better, more serious, than was that of Burnell. But it was saddening to discover that class and teachers receive no support – or books – from this country. They were getting their English from American writers such as John Cheever.

Like Burnell, I hunted the city for a postcard to send home. Like Burnell, I went to the railway station, on the line to Tashkent and beyond. Yes, this is the Golden Railroad to Samarkand! There I found the one and only postcard in all Ashgabat, faded, buckled, and printed with a four-kopek stamp – a symbol of the *ancien régime*, for Turkmenistan now has its own currency, the manat. I met the artist who designed the notes. Not a burdensome job, you might think, since all bore a certain chubby face.

The station features on the English jacket of *Somewhere East of Life*. The artist had never been there, any more than I had. Burnell found the place rather more lively than in fact it is.

My novel was published in August 1994, after I had returned from Turkmenistan. So what did I get right and what wrong? By and large, I gave that almost unknown country a better press than it has otherwise received. I am pleased to have brought it to readers' notice, and of course staggered by the way in which my interest found such a speedy response. What I got wrong mainly concerned religion, and there I had only a few sources to guide me.

The *Independent* Magazine ran a good article by Patrick Cockburn, but most information regarding the new Central Asian republics came from reports following the then US Secretary of State, James Baker's lightning visit there. These tended to be alarmist, implying that the states might embrace Islamic fundamentalism. Cockburn was more cautious. Following the American reports, I made Ashgabat more Muslim than I found to be the case.

After seventy years of Russian Communist rule, the Turkmen fell back on the mosque as many of us here in Britain fall on the church, at special occasions in our lives: christenings, weddings, and funerals. I saw no mosque, no minaret, in Ashgabat. It's true, I was sometimes greeted by a 'salaam alaikum'; on the other hand, they downed their vodka and wine like the veriest Moskovite atheist.

History-rich ground, and oil-rich, at that time, the future of Turkmenistan looked promising, although it was disconcerting to find how little was manufactured in the country; carpets and some textiles are exceptions. Streets were wide and well paved. Only pampered Europeans complained about the odd pothole. Among the Ladas rushing about, the new model Volvo 850s could be seen. The city, the entire state, depended on water from the Aral Sea. Every time you took a shower you were lowering the level of the doomed sea still further. The water flowed in through the Kara Kum Canal – the world's longest open ditch. Evaporation and seepage wasted a great deal; but, for a poor state, plans to install a water pipeline were impossibly extravagant.

My novel paints – how could it be otherwise? – a picture of a new place, a semi-imaginary Ashgabat. Some guesses were surprisingly accurate. Like Burnell, I found in Turkmenistan a world part rejoicing in, part regretting, their freedom from an order which had crumbled away, recently, unexpectedly, into the sands of history.

I came away feeling this was a place to be cherished, a place facing immense economic difficulties, but perhaps less extreme than its neighbours. And there was also some sadness. For, in what did these people believe? The building of new hotels is not a substitute for vision, especially with ten hotels standing empty. Yet Ashgabat seemed something of a triumph over adversity. The inhospitable dunes were held at bay, just beyond city limits. If anyone could make Mars habitable, the Turkmen could.

7

'It's the Disorientation I Relish'

'It's the Disorientation
I Relish'

A Revised Introduction to

The Penguin Science Fiction Omnibus

Science fiction stories are the fables of a technological age. Or let us suppose so for a while.

A tadpole in a pool bears little resemblance to the frog on land. Yet both are the same creature. A similar transformation can be seen in the history of science fiction. It is not only a literature in its own right; it proliferates on cinema screens and on small screens, it is prominent in computer games, where its startlements readily appeal to the young and not-so-young.

To say this is not to denigrate the written SF (let's use the family name for short); indeed, SF novels are more polished, embracing their outré scenarios more cunningly than ever before. Kissing cousins appear in the writing of Fay Weldon (*The Cloning of Joanna May*) and Kazuo Ishiguro (*Never Let Me Go*, for instance) and of course Doris Lessing's *Canopus in Argos* space fiction series of five novels – rather more of a full embrace than simply a kissing cousin. But there are fewer outlets, fewer magazines, for the short story than once there were. The great magazines were the monthly American *Astounding*, doyen of them all. The editor was John W. Campbell. Campbell had a degree in physics, but he also knew about How to Write. He said, 'If you have written a short story and can't think of a title, it's not a good story.' Profoundly true! Then came other grandees into the field, most notably *The Magazine of Fantasy and Science Fiction* and *Galaxy Magazine*. In England, the 1930s were gladdened by the Captain Justice stories of Murray Roberts. After the Second World War came *New Worlds*, edited by Ted Carnell. It was taken over by editor Michael Moorcock, who brought in new blood and new ideas. Now we have *Interzone* every month. And in my *Penguin Science Fiction Omnibus* are displayed some of these briefer virtuoso performances.

So no neighbourly Jorge Luis Borges, no cousinly Franz Kafka, despite their rather similar function to disorientate the reader. I was once in a New York restaurant where two elderly judges were sitting at the next table. They were well into their cocktails. One judge was trying to explain to the other judge what Kafka's *Trial* was about. He seemed as puzzled as the other guy.

I first came across John Crowley's magnificent short story 'Great Work of Time' in one of the anthologies by my wise friend David Hartwell. It is hardly a story which could have been written or published, I think, before the 1980s. Or if written, then not published, since editors felt they had their responsibilities to cling to a familiar line of goods. Its parts come gradually together, as the story itself says. It includes the Bulawayo Railway Bridge, what angels might call themselves when alone, one Denys entering 'a precinct outside time', and *bons mots* such as 'You're not in possession of any secret, only a madman's certainty.'

It was first published in 1989. Playful, serious, astonishing: it's a brilliant individual piece of storytelling. Certain that we don't know for certain what we are about. It's one of science fiction's elusive beauties, as you could say of Robert Holdstock's *Mythago Wood*, or of Olaf Stapledon's grave, aloof, *Star Maker*.

Subject matter has changed over the years, as one might expect. The technocratic emphasis of the fictions prevailing in the 1940s and 1950s – hardly surprisingly in wartime and Cold War time – has become diluted. Lowering the technocratic threshold appears to account for its wider readership among women readers nowadays. As an academic remarked to me, 'I'm not interested in the machinery: it's the disorientation I relish.' Disorientation is what I was seeking in my story, 'Poor Little Warrior', written in a style known (or unknown) as 'Barbaric-Trendy'. We have to be prepared for Tiny Fates when we have overcome all the big ones . . .

Reviewing *The Penguin Science Fiction Omnibus* in the *TLS* (2008), Professor Dinah Birch remarks on this development while saying how SF 'allows them (writers and readers) to find subtle ways of exploring cultural anxiety and desire'. As we leave behind the frosty air of the Cold War, innovative modes of SF reflect on numerous things Birch mentions, including the nature of religion, the relationships between animals and humanity, and so on.

In an October 2006 issue of the same paper, the reviewer, Michael Saler, devotes a page to an examination of the fiction and life of James Tiptree Jr. Tiptree's fiction appeared first in SF magazines in the late 1960s and was immediately recognized as speaking with a powerful new voice, discoursing sometimes obliquely on dark sexual subjects ('mankind is exogamous', as in the story in my anthology). It was not until 1976 that readers discovered that Tiptree was in fact a woman, a 60-year-old, by name Alice Bradley Sheldon. The contained melancholy of Tiptree's story, 'And I Awoke and Found Me Here on the Cold Hill's Side', delivers some of the troubles besetting the human spirit. 'He took a breath, consulting some vast disarray of the soul,' she/he says. And we understand.

Sheldon decided rather late in life she needed to write SF. I am reminded of an incident with my father, Stanley Aldiss. He was a Gent's Outfitter, in charge of a large emporium in East Dereham, Norfolk. One day, he put an arm on my shoulder and said, with a sweep of his hand, 'One day, all this will be yours.' My blood froze. I did not want it, nor had I any interest in it. I knew I was going to be a writer: perhaps if I was good enough, tormented enough, I would become a science fiction writer! Certainly I was already on nodding acquaintance with the disarray of the soul of which Tiptree speaks.

Alice Sheldon wrote to a friend, 'Those eight years in SF were the first time I could be really real.' Such sentiments contain what drives a writer to SF, as well as what drives SF on. For whatever reasons, we are discontented with the world-as-is. SF stories indicate our dissatisfaction with our station in life, our laws, our presidents, the assumptions our parents presume to make for us, the nigh-insane quest for 'happiness' which may yet ruin our civilization – or indeed a thousand other aspects of life. We are the Steppen-wolves of our culture. We live in that culture, in general as law-abiding citizens, but we occasionally speak – as Tiptree spoke, largely in metaphor – of different worlds, utopias, or dystopias, Brave New Worlds or 1984s. And we bring them, we hope, to grotesque or logical conclusions, just as our very beings are composed of particles from infinitely distant stellar explosions, distant in both space and time; we have come to understand that we also are grotesque and logical continuations of a mighty universal process. Many readers miss something by not adapting themselves to the mode we have found the need, like Tiptree, to adopt, and the distances from the mundane we explore.

An ideal and delicious example is William Tenn's story, 'The Liberation of Earth'. It was first published in an obscure magazine in 1953, which superior custodians of our literature would have been shocked even to see.

Of course the sad tale of Earth's increasing desolation is funny, in Tenn's best ironic manner. But if we think of 'liberation' as 'regime change', we perceive its continuing topicality, an adroit use of distancing metaphor.

When I was first collecting these stories, back in the 1960s, my friend and competitor, Edmund Crispin, was also compiling SF anthologies. Crispin got to Fredric Brown's story, 'Answer', first. While attending a *New Scientist* party at about that time, I heard one young scientist telling another the story of 'Answer'. It was clear he had not read the story himself; someone had told it to him. He was passing it on. It had achieved escape velocity from the printed page. It had evolved into a fable.

I began by claiming that SF stories are the fables of our time. 'Answer' was one story in particular I was thinking about: the birth of a new god! For the opening of a great new computer, the President of the Worlds is invited to ask a single question. He asks if there is a God. The answer is unexpected – and shocking. But movies, too, function in the same way. *Planet of the Apes* concludes with Charlton Heston finding the Statue of Liberty destroyed, half-buried in the sands. 'You fools, damn you, you finally did it!' With that pained condemnation of nuclear warfare, the film makes clear all that has gone before. So it closes.

Of course, things are not always sobersided. The use of irony often comes to our aid. When my history of science fiction, *Billion Year Spree,* was first published in 1973, I used a cut on its yellow jacket showing planes roaring over New York, blasting skyscrapers, setting them on fire. That picture had formed part of the cover of a magazine entitled Stories of *Super Science*. This magazine bore an enticing tagline, 'Read It Today! Live It Tomorrow!'

As indeed we did on 9/11.

'Read it today – live it yesterday' could well be a tagline for stories of enduring popularity read before the label 'science fiction' was current. In the early decades of the eighteenth century appeared Daniel Defoe's *Robinson Crusoe* (1719), to be followed a little later by Jonathan Swift's *Gulliver's Travels* (1726). As I say elsewhere, these immense successes are still read today, a study of a man cast up on an alien planet, and a story of big and little aliens, and horses that speak. Roughly speaking, of course.

Another brilliant example of the fantastic emerges with Bulwer-Lytton's *The Coming Race*, published in 1871. A whole civilization, living underground, plans to emerge, not entirely unlike H.G. Wells's morlocks, a generation or more later. Lytton's submerged society has no electricity; instead there is the all-pervasive 'vryl', an immense source of energy.

Britain was then the centre of world industry. On the domestic front, many new luxuries were becoming available. The misgivings of a new threat emerging from below had a Freudian touch. In any case, the story was so immensely popular that a new table delicacy was named Bovril. Vryl was also used in the christening of a new toffee-type medicament for growing lads. I enjoyed it myself as a boy; it was called Vyrol!

Here, I have space only for British and American writing. For those interested in what was happening on the Continent, one might consult the Italian *Storia della Fantascienza*, edited by Ugo Malaguti, or the grand French *Encyclopédie de l'Utopie des Voyages Extraordinaires et de la Science Fiction*, edited by Pierre Versins. Of course, if you are into collecting encyclopaedias, the authoritative volume is *The Encyclopaedia of Science Fiction*, edited by John Clute.

SF has become more domestic of late. This is in part because young writers have grown older and have settled down. Our western world has an immense variety of adventures, improvements, miseries and speculations from which we can make our choice. Yes, we can take in the dark side of our culture, but it helps if we know the dark side of Central Asia as well.

As an old hand at this game, I find myself missing the plethora of stories set on other planets and in outer space, which were once the backbone of recent SF. Distance and dislocation were always pleasurable to encounter. But we have come to realize how difficult it is even to manage the hop to neighbouring Mars.

Isaac Asimov, a clever and engaging writer, was heard to remark, after Neil Armstrong set foot on the Moon, that this event justified all the SF written since 1940. The comment is invalid: invalid in more than one respect (for instance, the misunderstanding that SF is a united entity, rather than diverse in content and temperament); behind it lies Asimov's assumption that SF was an instrument of prediction. This was – again – the technocratic emphasis of SF. Ever since Apollo 11 and the landing on the Moon, the emphasis, the very conception, of SF has changed; our weather vane points more in the direction of metaphor.

Writing my first SF novel, *Non-Stop*, about people imprisoned in circumstances beyond their control and knowing nothing of the world, I was conscious of reconstructing on one level my own confining circumstances. Such is the power of metaphor that my novel became extremely popular in the Poland of that time, where it was read as a coded criticism of the Communist regime within which that society was imprisoned.

It may be this metaphorical quality of the discourse that permits science fiction to travel round the globe – a freedom hardly attainable for a novel set in, let's say, Croydon. While that novel might flourish in Croydon, it would probably go unheeded in Paris and Tokyo.

James Inglis's story of grand despair and infinite space, 'Night Watch', is, as far as we can discover, the one and only story Inglis ever wrote. Possibly he felt a Tiptree-like urge to escape from himself, to live in a universe free of humanity. 'On his way, the Automatic Stellar Observation Vehicle charted the downfall of the galaxy. He observed each dead and dying star which came within his long-range senses. Very occasionally he approached close enough to witness the funeral processions of whole solar systems.' We can only speculate on whether the story proved in some way to be curative for him. In any case, it is a pure Steppenwolf story.

SF used to have a small sister, a sweet little creature with pearls in her hair and stars in her eyes. She grew up to be a big brawny lass, threatening her parents and staying out late at night. Her name is Fantasy. Sometimes Fantasy and SF blend – a mating one might expect. But there is an important distinction to be made between the twain. A fantasy story – J.R.R. Tolkien provides an example always to hand – tends to end happily with an evil defeated and the world going back to the way it used to be. A conservative ending.

In a really good SF story – and we might have Greg Bear's 'Blood Music' in mind – the world is changed. Evil may be repulsed, but the world can never return to what it was before. Here again we think of 9/11. A revolutionary ending.

Change is the great subject for SF, power and change. The story by Eliza Blair, 'Friends in Need', written when Blair was a student at Swarthmore College, is an excellent example of this. Even the language has morphed itself, becoming more to resemble a text message.

It was in an SF magazine that I first encountered the word 'ecology'. For many years I have admired James Schmitz's story, 'Grandpa'. Here's ecology with a vengeance, as this large vegetable structure, Grandpa itself, heads off to mate in the surly embrace of the Zlanti Deeps. Ah, those chill Zlanti Deeps – how long they haunted me!

Harry Harrison's story, as with 'Grandpa', is set on another planet. Here we are, in a world where the indigenous people are, in Garth's words, 'The only primitive people I have ever encountered who are free of superstition, and appear to be much happier and saner because of it.' It's a good teasing idea – had the writer the Bible in mind?

Never can an SF story be too extreme, or too foreign, for me. 'Swarm', by Bruce Sterling, presents another guaranteed extreme, possibly hard at first fully to grasp. Captain-Doctor Afriel meets a hostile Swarm in the asteroid belt. His large intestine has been altered to reproduce the vitamins normally made by intestinal bacteria. So we enter the gruesome and complex world of the Swarm. This is an argument about civilization itself, and its power to endure. The story is horrifying.

I listen to stories read on BBC Radio 4, the star radio channel, and it has always surprised me that they never select a story from the wealth of science fiction's treasury. Their stories mainly concern tales of unhappy Irish childhoods, or two people meeting in Bedford, with bittersweet but conventional results. I would trade them all for one dip in the Zlanti Deeps! How one longs for a more impassioned approach, with the imagination kicked about a little! It is imagination that has created the world of the West – imagination and its cousin, ingenuity. We should grant it more respect. Ought we not to think better of a liking for the far-fetched?

However, ignorance and the cold-shouldering of the medium and its cousins is of long-standing. I have four histories of French literature on my shelves; they are rather past their sell-by date, admittedly, but none of them gives so much as a mention to Jules Verne. Poor Jules, whom the Pope blessed for his writing.

Can a withholding of enthusiasm be because it is 'only about imaginary things'? Imagination is a vital quality; children swim in it much of the time, as when they talk to their teddy bears, their plastic plesiosaurs. An attempt to describe how imagination functions is made by the Oxford philosopher Mary Warnock in her book entitled *Imagination*.

Warnock believes strongly that the cultivation of imagination should be the chief aim of education. Later, she says:

[T]here is a power in the human mind which is at work in our everyday perception of the world, and which is also at work in our thoughts about what is absent; which enables us to see the world, whether present or absent, as significant, and also to present this vision to others to share or reject. And this power . . . is not only intellectual. Its impetus comes from the emotions as much as from the reason, from the heart as much as from the head.

We might also consider that we earthlings are moving at about eighteen miles per second with terrestrial rotation, not to mention our haste to keep up with the galaxy; these little-discerned velocities may cause disturbances of which we remain ignorant – and for which there is no cure. Little wonder our lives are short and hasty!

So, we might regard as preposterous the statement in Fredric Brown's 'Answer', that there are 96 billion civilized planets in the universe: that does not detract from the power of the story, which depends not so much on science as on our fear of being dominated by an omnipotent being.

Indeed, if we wish to know how many civilized planets there are in the universe, we can read, for instance, the book by George Basalla, entitled *Civilized Life in the Universe* (2006), and we shall be chastised and enlightened by his learned answer to the question. More recent, more challenging, is Stephen Hawking's *The Grand Design* (2010), which discusses much requiring attention, including the existence of multiple universes.

So long neglected when confined mainly to the printing press, that vital invention of an earlier age, SF awaited newer media to attain a wider popularity. The decor – the very environment which is often the most vital 'character' of an SF story – demanded the birth of the electronic age, which created both wide- and small-screen viewing. SF movies are now so popular that they no longer bother to announce themselves as 'SF', or as the slummy nickname, 'sci-fi'. This trend may have been prompted by a modern masterpiece of the screen and of the genre, *The Truman Show*, directed by Peter Weir.

Sometimes such movies are occasioned by a new technological development and can be otherwise idea-free (*Terminator 2* is an example). If a movie meets with success it is quite likely to have a sequel made, and possibly more than one; safety insurance and limited budgets are enemies of creativity. Thus the Oscar-winning *Planet of the Apes* (1963), to which reference has already been made, was followed by four sequels, as well as two TV series. Not surprisingly, none had the pungency, or of course the originality, of the first drama.

We all know that franchises are hard to resist. Another example begins with the brilliant *Alien*, directed by the astonishing Ridley Scott (*Thelma and Louise*, for example, had Scott as director). It has Sigourney Weaver fighting the aliens and John Hurt giving birth to one via his chest. Two sequels have followed, actually quite worth watching. In space, no audiences can be heard screaming.

Some older facets of SF remain and I hope always will: the ingenuity of Eric Frank Russell's 'Sole Solution', the penetrating moral of Jack Chandler's 'The Cage', the terror of Walter Miller's take on 'Frankenstein', entitled 'I Made You', and of course the cosmic awe of Inglis's 'Night Watch'. Such fables as these have earned preservation.

Yet the USA remains the Mecca. Americans are better at science fiction than anyone else. A customs officer at JFK airport, checking my passport, recognized my name and said, 'Welcome to America – everyone reads SF here.' One can only imagine the same thing happening at Heathrow.

94

8

The Gulag
Archipelago

The Gulag Archipelago

Alexander Solzhenitsyn's *The Gulag Archipelago* begins with dreadful power:

> Hour by hour planes fly there, ships steer their course there, and trains thunder off to it – but all with nary a mark on them to tell of their destination. And at ticket windows or at travel bureaus for Soviet or foreign tourists the employees would be astounded if you were to ask for a ticket to go there . . . And those who, like you and me, dear reader, go there to die, must get there solely and compulsorily via arrest.

It's like the opening of a great SF trilogy, and certainly of a latter-day Tolstoy novel. But the world of the Gulag, though dreamed up by demented minds, was real enough. It still remains a monument to human cruelty – although this great and determined man, who died in 2008 at the age of 89, has a coda to that, which we shall come to.

Solzhenitsyn was dispatched to the notorious Gulag Archipelago in 1945 for writing a letter in which he criticized Joseph Stalin as 'the man with the moustache'.

He served in the punishment camps and prisons near Moscow, and in a camp in Ekibastuz, Kazakhstan (1945–53). During these years, his double degree in mathematics and physics saved him mostly from hard physical labour in that most atrocious of places. He returned like one returning from the dead.

By the end of Book II, if we have survived its terrors, we are startled by the chapter entitled 'Ascent', in which we learn how the camp system and its bitter labours can be endured: how indeed it can refurbish our souls. This man speaks with authority; his theme will reveal the ultimate triumph of the human spirit over a hostile ideology.

The way to these inhuman labour camps which stretched across the Soviet Union began with a night arrest. They hammered at your door and that was the beginning. That process and those processes which followed were designed to frighten and demolish the will of the innocent as well as the guilty. Once the prison doors closed, you were on your way.

The labour camps, often established within the Arctic Circle, contained all sorts and conditions of men and women – of prisoners, zeks and zechka, much like the prisons in Tolstoy's novel, *Resurrection*.

In an island of the archipelago called Ekibastuz, in the squalor of a labour camp, Solzhenitsyn walked with a fellow zek. This zek was a religious poet called Silin, whom Solzhenitsyn had just met. Silin worked as a manual labourer and ditch-digger. He recited a long religious poem he had composed in his head.

Not a word of the poem had been written down. Written? What with? There was no pencil, no paper, to be had within a thousand miles. Silin has by heart, Solzhenitsyn estimated, some twenty thousand lines. It was Solzhenitsyn's regret that – with his brain full of his own unwritten verse – he remembered only two dozen or so lines of Silin's long poem. Those fragments he quoted in *The Gulag Archipelago*, so that something, something may survive from Silin's tormented life.

One couplet runs as follows:

> . . . That though Christ's teaching is its theme
> Genius must ever speak with its own voice.
>
> *(III, p. 107; references are to The Folio Society edition, 2005,*
> *translated by Thomas P. Whitney and Harry Willetts)*

These three volumes which spell out the Soviet Union's horrifying history form a supreme example of genius speaking with its own voice. We indeed come to believe that such travails as he describes move – it is a very Russian thought – 'in the direction of deepening the soul' (II, p. 604). Although this statement is alien to our way of life in the West, with the triviality of our pop idols, there surely are many who ruefully admit to this truth, and understand how hardship fortifies us. It does not make us laugh, it does not fill us with glee. There may indeed be truth in what Lesley Blanch claims in her extraordinary volume, *The Sabres of Paradise*, about Russia's troubles with Chechnya, which continue to this day: 'the atmosphere of gentle gloom,' she says, 'that heady draught of romanticized melancholy which only the East knows how to distill, and which, once tasted by the West, is forever craved'. Silin's lost twenty thousand lines of verse are of that category.

The Gulag Archipelago was established in Lenin's time, when prisons overflowed and more places of incarceration were needed. Those prisoners, like Solzhenitsyn himself, needed no ticket; you reached the archipelago, as he says, solely by arrest. This clandestine system of destructive labour camps stretched for thousands of miles, from the vicinity of Moscow itself all the way to Vladivostok on the Pacific coast, and from Kazakhstan and what is now Kyrgyzstan in the south to far into the Arctic Circle, to Murmansk and Kolyma in the north, where intense cold allied itself to injustice against those serving out their punishment there.

In his youth, Alexander Solzhenitsyn had been a student and admirer of Lenin. He came to despise him as the man who paved the way for the monstrous Stalin.

In Russia, there had been civil war, beginning in 1917, leading to the establishment of a Bolshevik government under Lenin. It was in August 1918 that Lenin gave the order to 'carry out merciless mass terror' (II, p. 17). It remains almost unthinkable! The Red Terror spawned the Cheka, which owed nothing to legality. The Cheka later became in turn the GPU, the OGPU, the NKVD, and the KGB. Under all these later names Solzhenitsyn knew well this remorseless organization, which flourished like ground elder, inerradicable, throughout the years of the Soviet Union.

Filthy prisons and exile to Siberia had existed in the centuries of the tzars. These were rapidly developed under pressure of numbers, as innocent and guilty alike were swept into the maw of the Terror. Monasteries such as Solovetsky, not too far from Archangel, were taken over as prisons, the monks being without ceremony kicked out to perish of starvation and cold.

The night arrest, as we have seen, began that inevitable journey: 'There is where the Gulag country begins, right next to us, two yards away from us' (I, p. 4). Solzhenitsyn is the Virgil who leads us down into the chilliest circles of hell. With him we enter a world system of unspeakable cruelty and unimaginable suffering. Everything truthful languished. When first arrested, the prisoner's mind was in confusion. Solzhenitsyn confesses, 'We did not love freedom enough . . . We submitted with pleasure!' (I, p. 13).

Maybe it was a mistake, this arrest, and would be sorted out later. But nothing is ever sorted out: guilt and innocence are out-of-date concepts (I, p. 76). 'We are interrogated, denied sleep, starved and interrogated again. It is almost with joy that we gain our first cell . . .' At Solovetsky the monks die, the model agricultural enterprise is destroyed (II, p. 49); the very vegetables are tainted by Christianity.

But at least prisoners are incarcerated in a good stone building.

Most prisoners were not so fortunate. Many were sent to live in tents in sub-zero temperatures. Many were driven deeper into the wilderness to build their own camps, and slept out in the open while they did so. In the tundra and taiga arose hundreds of these vile camps, in which men laboured, starved, perished (II, p. 73). To starvation rations were added insane work demands.

Here's a case. In Shalamov on the Kolyma river, the summer work day was sixteen hours long. There was also the three-hour walk to the forest, the work site, and three hours back again. If the norm was not fulfilled, then the zek sloggers were left in the forest to work by the light of searchlights. They returned to camp just before morning. They ate their dinner with their breakfast, before having to return immediately to the woods. They all died (II, p. 201). Amid the indifferent forests, by the indifferent waters of the indifferent river, there was no mercy; compassion had been legislated against. Beria was put in overall command, Lavrenti Beria, at one time the second most powerful person in the USSR.

In a rather guarded chapter, the author deals with the zechka, the lives of women in the camps. Fruitless indignation and belated regret prompt one to endure many more details of the barbarism inflicted on the two and a half million female inmates of the camps, but Solzhenitsyn himself is the supreme chronicler of the various ways in which the human personality was 'dissolving . . . into faeces and ash' (II, p. 208). All this at a time when the liars at the top of the pile were busy inventing Homo Sovieticus, the supreme Soviet Man!

> Words are not enough, for this human being cannot be made to fit into mere formulae . . . He is first of all a Man of Labour . . . He is a man of lofty ideals . . . He is a man about whom the state cares a great deal . . . Cities grow, green parks abound, new goods are put on the market, scientists are concerned about clean air – and all this is for him, for Soviet Man, and free of charge or at very little cost to himself.
>
> *(From an article in* Sovetskye lyudi, *quoted in Mikhail Heller,* Cogs in the Soviet Wheel: The Formation of Soviet Man, *p. 47)*

We turn to examine the rot that spread like gangrene from the camps, to poison the entire Soviet system, the escape valve of tukhta (II, pp. 163–7).

Tukhta began in one of the logging camps, where the zeks were required to fulfil exacting work norms during a particularly hard winter. They managed only 60 per cent of the norms. Nevertheless, they were rewarded by increased rations for having met, it was claimed, 125 per cent of their norms. This conjuring trick was managed by Vasily Vlasov, the planner of the camp and a zek himself.

The camp chief investigated this fictitious output, and discovered the considerable shortfall of the claimed quota of timber. He was furious. But Vlasov drew up a document which 'found' all the missing timber. The enquiries came from higher-ups: where was this timber? The chief raged, but Vlasov said, 'Wait till the roads have dissolved in mud.'

At that juncture, he prepared a report stating that the highly successful logging operation had rendered it impossible to move the 10,500 cubic yards of timber out of the swampy forests. He gave an estimate for the cost of building a road to the timber, showing that such a road, together with the haulage required, would cost more than the timber was worth. Moreover, since the logs were going to be lying in the swamp all summer, they would be unsuitable for lumber. The administration had no alternative but to accept this report. The doomed trees remained upright. The zeks received those extra rations of black bread. Many lives were saved.

Yields were always inflated from then on. The log-rafting office also had its problems. It too had impossible norms to achieve. So it accepted the inflated figure from the camp and freighted the fictitious timber downriver. At the sorting point downriver, again zeks were in charge. They too had their impossible norms to fulfil. They too needed an extra crust. They accepted the fictitious timber – and added a bit more on their own account.

Next came the sawmill, also run by zeks. They were bound to protect their pals upstream. They too had their own needs. So the inflated figure was passed on. The lie flew. The fictitious lumber was locked up in the lumber yard. Then interminable delays entered, whereby lumber 'spoiled' and became unfit for delivery. And many mouths were fed.

Eventually, the grand shortfall reached the State Planning Commission, which sent an enquiry back to Vlasov. But there were countless such papers in circulation. Things got lost in the fudge of criminal confusion. The Ministry for the Timber Industry was forced to use the fictitious figures in its reports. It also had its requirements. Thus, the fiction of tukhta permeated the nation.

As Solzhenitsyn says, in one of his great-hearted phrases, 'Not even the Commission could stand up against people's pressure to live. All this was a matter of attempting to survive, not to enrich oneself, and certainly not to plunder the state' (II, p. 166). It was the state which had forced this massive deception on itself.

Due to all these contributory causes, Solzhenitsyn remarks, sarcastically, 'Not only does the Archipelago not pay its own way, but the nation has to pay dearly for the additional satisfaction of having it' (II, p. 587).

In the face of this insatiable cancer, the famine in Ukraine in the early 1930s became like a mere detail, although careful estimates indicated there were some 5 million deaths from hunger and the diseases starvation brings. Robert Conquest places blame for the famine directly on Stalin: 'It is also the only major famine whose very existence was ignored or denied by the governmental authorities.' Conquest relates how Stalin tells Churchill that 10 million kulaks (rich peasants) were 'dealt with' — many of them transferred to Siberia, to perish in the camps. As for machine power on the collectivized farms, it amounted to less in 1938 than it had been in 1929. A tractor shortage prevailed; and half of Russia's horses had been slaughtered during the first Five-Year Plan.

The third volume of Solzhenitsyn's massive work deals with the war years, when, naturally enough, conditions for the katorzhane, the workforce, became harder. Here are thrilling stories of escape and endurance. From later chapters emerges the theme of exile. 'Here we see that the threat of exile . . . has a sombre power of its own, the power which even ancient potentates understood, and which Ovid long ago experienced. Emptiness. Helplessness. A life that is no life at all . . .' (III, p. 340).

Whole villages at a time were sent to be devoured by exile. The plight of one body of peasants, which Solzhenitsyn instances differed in kind from all previous exiles (III, p. 362). They were banished to a wilderness, into mankind's primitive condition. The Cheka planted these special settlements on stony hillsides, where nothing would grow, far from the river Pinega. Solzhenitsyn points out that a peasant's life was usually spent surrounded by animals. 'Here he was condemned for many years never to hear neighing or lowing or bleating, never to saddle, never to milk, never to fill a trough.'

Many special settlements died off to the last man and woman. Where those settlements once stood, tourists now kick the skulls out of sight. In other dreadful places, as many as seventy thousand people were driven on foot in deepest winter to a remote place, given no food or tools, to fend for themselves as best they could. They all perished.

Exile. Even those of us forced to spend years of our youth in the Far East, away from our home country, feel forever its impact on our return. How much more severe for zeks! Zeks who survived long harsh terms of punishment went – as did Solzhenitsyn – into exile. He arrived at first in a place called Karaganda, where penniless exiles lived out their lives in corridors, dark box-like rooms, or in sheds. The wilder the places of exile, the worse things were. Strangely enough, life in exile was harder than life in the camps. An exile lived as a timorous recluse. 'There were none of those long intimate conversations, those confessions of things past, usual in prisons and camps' (III, p. 383).

It was an accepted saying that everything was possible in the Gulag (II, p. 468). The blackest foulness, any twist or turn of betrayal, wildly unexpected encounters, love on the edge of the precipice – everything was possible. But we stumble on the truth of it: 'there is nothing funny in our life; everything funny takes place in the West' (II, p. 584).

Whole nations were sent into cheerless exile. We note that Solzhenitsyn singles out for comment the Chechens as the 'one nation that would not give in, would not acquire the mental habits of submission. The Chechens never sought to please . . . their attitude was always haughty and indeed openly hostile.' Perhaps they were nourished on folk memories of Tolstoy's *The Cossacks*, or of the Murad Wars, fought in the early nineteenth century, when Dagestan, close neighbour of Chechnya, withstood the forces of the tzar: when Shamyl, Imam of Dagestan, defied Emperor Nicholas I, in the bitter conflict portrayed by Lesley Blanch in her *Sabres of Paradise*.

Solzhenitsyn was exiled to Kazakhstan, where he rented a henhouse with one dirty window and a low roof. He began to write. On one occasion during his long stay, he went to the central square. People, mainly old, were gathered there. An announcement was coming over the radio loudspeaker. It was 5 March 1953. Joseph Stalin is dead! 'The villain has curled up and died!' (III, p. 421).

Young girls and schoolteachers were crying, asking what was to become of them. Solzhenitsyn kept a straight face, perfected in his days as a zek. He has learnt the rule of his life: 'Do not rejoice when you have found, do not weep when you have lost' (II, p. 611).

Soon Lavrenti Beria was deposed – he had become Minister of the Interior since the Great One's death. While the MGB became the KGB, the repercussions in the camps were great. A thaw was setting in. Some prisoners were even allowed to go home. Even exiles were treated more politely.

An entire Kazak school class was entrusted to Solzhenitsyn's care and teaching. He entered into the task with enthusiasm, trying to spread a little enlightenment – as he succeeds in doing in this, his greatest book. And all the while he was teaching, he was writing and writing, striving to compile this dread document.

As Solzhenitsyn admits, 'This is not a very cheery book' (II, p. 478). But when he, a survivor, comes to reflect on his experiences, his conclusions are perhaps surprising to us in the West.

In a chapter entitled 'The Ascent', he makes this statement:

Your soul, which formerly was dry, now ripens from suffering. And even if you have not come to love your neighbours in the Christian sense, you are at least coming to love those close to you. Those close to you in spirit are who surround you in slavery. And how many of us come to realise: it is particularly in slavery that for the first time we have learned to recognise genuine friendship! (II, p. 611)

A long meditation follows. Then comes:

It was granted to me to carry away from my prison years on my bent back, which nearly broke beneath its load, this essential experience: how a human being becomes evil and how good . . . Since then, I have come to understand the truth of all the religions of the world: they struggle with the evil inside a human being. It is impossible to expel evil from the world in its entirety, but it is possible to constrict it within each person.

According to Michael Scammell, Solzhenitsyn got the news that he had won the Nobel Prize from a cleaner. This was in October 1970. He had already been expelled from the Writers Union. What a furore the news stirred up in Moscow! A poet called Abashidze said, 'I have seen few people as insolent as Solzhenitsyn. Our government is very tolerant of such a scoundrel.'

Shortly following the publication of *Gulag,* Solzhenitsyn was expelled from the Soviet Union. The date was 13 February 1974. An Aeroflot plane landed him in Frankfurt, Germany. As he reached the door of the plane, his plane escort thrust 500 marks into his hand – a parting present from the KGB.

The difficulties which had to be overcome to effect the birth of this mighty work were formidable: first, to the preservation of Solzhenitsyn's papers; then with regard to the collecting of data and reminiscence in primitive conditions; then defiance of state persecution; then the problems of translation; and finally with the act of publishing in various countries. Only a man of Solzhenitsyn's stubborn and combative temperament could have overcome such pyramids of impediment.

The first volume of *Gulag* was published by Harper and Row, in the USA, in 1973, translated from the Russian by Thomas P. Whitney. Other volumes followed, the third being translated by H.T. Willetts. This same translation was published in England by Collins and Harvill Press shortly afterwards.

The Gulag Archipelago is a magnificent and courageous book, its most harrowing passages etched by a purgative intention. What would otherwise be unbearable resounds with the fortitude, spirit and intellect which have forged this desolate stretch of recent history into a whole intense experience. Certainly *The Gulag Archipelago* is a history. It is also literature; Solzhenitsyn was versed in the great Russian novelists. His frequent mode of scathing sarcasm matches a great deal we find also in Leo Tolstoy's extraordinary third novel, *Resurrection,* where the false facades of society are stripped away. *Gulag* is a long and vivid meditation on the good and evil in human hearts. We who live out our lives in better circumstances must still confront its relevance. There is no book like it in the world.

9

The Continuing War of the Worlds

The Continuing
War of the Worlds

In the middle of the seventeenth century, the Dutch son of a basket-maker made an alarming discovery. His name was Antony van Leeuwenhoek. He ground his own lenses and constructed a microscope. Whereas Galileo had been surveying the stars and Isaac Newton had been measuring the Moon's orbit, van Leeuwenhoek looked in the opposite direction, into the very small.

Observing a drop of water from a lake, he found it full of living things, of 'animalcules'. 'On these last I saw two little legs near the head, and two little fins at the hindmost end of the body . . . And the motion of most of these animalcules in the water was so swift, and so various upwards, downwards, and round about, that 'twas wonderful to see.'

At last, someone had discovered alien life!

Long before the seventeenth century, the human mind was amply populated by hobgoblins of all kinds, and indeed still continues to be. Ghosts and vampires abound there. But to discover these minute and seemingly hostile 'animalcules' in a drop of water was a new and disquieting thing. Water! Water, the symbol of purity, infested with unimagined creatures! Peace of mind departs and one more step towards our neurotic modern world is taken.

The young Mr H.G. Wells attended the biological laboratory of what was in 1884 known as the Normal School of Science. An echo of his learning experience sounds in the opening lines of his short story, 'The Stolen Bacillus'. 'This again', said the Bacteriologist, slipping a glass slide under the microscope, 'is a preparation of the celebrated bacillus of cholera – the cholera germ.'

The ubiquity of 'germs' as an idea took hold on Wells's mind.

Herbert George Wells was born in 1866, of lower-middle-class parents. The parents ran a china shop in Bromley, in Kent. At the age of seven, young Bertie broke his leg and was laid up for weeks. Sympathy and books came his way, so perhaps it was a lucky accident.

Although the population of Bromley increased from twenty thousand to fifty thousand in the decades of the 1960s, 1970s and 1980s, it seems that none of the new inhabitants wanted to buy any china. The shop closed amid an increased urban sprawl which continues today.

Wells's education included a spell under the great scientist and humanist, Thomas Huxley. Huxley, in his vigorous defence of Darwin's evolutionary theory, became known as 'Darwin's Bulldog'. His grandsons included Julian and Aldous Huxley. Once Wells had won his hard-earned freedom, he moved ever onwards; through over a hundred books, we see him struggling with questions of evolution, over-population, education, and the betterment of humankind.

He became a leading contributor to the Sankey Declaration of the Rights of Man, which later formed part of the charter of the United Nations. When the UN General Assembly held its first session in London in January 1946, Wells was in his last months of life. He died peacefully on 13 August of that year.

His creative powers had waned as his strength as a polemicist grew. In his early novels, these aspects are in balance: and never more so than in *The War of the Worlds*. The novel's thrilling and horrific theme aims to puncture mankind's pretensions. As the 1930s dawn, novels give way to treatises, such as 'The Way to World Peace' (1930), 'The Work, Wealth and Happiness of Mankind' (1932), 'World Brain' (1938), and 'The Fate of Homo Sapiens' (1939).

It was a part of Wells's genius that he could invent things never before imagined. A character in Chekhov's play, *The Seagull*, says, 'We should show life neither as it is nor as it ought to be, but as we see it in our dreams.' It's the Surrealists' prescription and one at which Wells was good in his early days, until he began desiring to change the world – by force if necessary. We see a foreshadowing of this wish at the conclusion of *The War of the Worlds*, when the narrator tells us that the Martians have done much to 'promote the conception of the commonweal of mankind'.

117

But to say this is to begin at the end. To begin at the beginning, and at that magnificent paragraph with which *The War of the Worlds* opens, we find mention of 'a man with a microscope' who might scrutinize 'the transient creatures that swarm and multiply in a drop of water' (p. 9; references are to the Penguin Classics edition, 2005). We shall find that this first reference, hardly cordial, to mankind as a whole is to be followed by many other unflattering descriptions.

I first came upon this novel at a youthful age, when I was not unfamiliar with the more conventional novels to which the term 'classics' was applied. Among such novels were *Robinson Crusoe*, *Oliver Twist*, and *Jane Eyre*. But I do not recall any sentence which ever had such an awesome effect on me as one sentence in that first paragraph of *The War of the Worlds*: 'Yet across the gulf of space, minds that are to our minds as ours are to those of the beasts that perish, intellects vast and cool and unsympathetic, regarded this earth with envious eyes, and slowly and surely drew their plans against us.' Had there ever been such an opening statement, labyrinthine yet pellucid, before? No latinate long words here, designed to impress; the longest word is that readily comprehensible understatement of an adjective, 'unsympathetic'.

So the curtain comes up on the drama, and already the seeds of Wells's clever denouement have been planted.

The novel was published in hardcover in 1898, having been serialized in a popular magazine in 1897, the year of a second Victorian jubilee and much British self-congratulation. The later decades of the nineteenth century had seen the popularity of the Sensation Novel, 'read alike in drawing-room and kitchen'. Such novels might concern adultery or bigamy, famous examples of both being *Lady Audley's Secret* and *East Lynn* (wherein the famous line occurs, 'Dead – and never called me mother!') Something of the ubiquity of these novels was owed to the 1871 Bill to provide public elementary education for all. The Education Act marks the first time that the state assumed direct responsibility for general education. A new readership developed, open to the wonders of Mr H.G. Wells.

There are sensations more overwhelming than adultery, more terrible than bigamy. The sensations of warfare and societal change in which Wells trafficked also emerge in the late decades of the nineteenth century. The year 1871 alone brought Bulwer-Lytton's *The Coming Race*, Samuel Butler's *Erewhon*, and Colonel George Chesney's *The Battle of Dorking*. The latter pamphlet describes a German invasion of England. England, unprepared, is defeated by Germany.

The story created an immediate effect, popular and political. The device of future war, and sudden invasion, which exposes the unprepared nation to inevitable defeat, aroused fears and imitations everywhere. As Professor I.F. Clarke puts it in his invaluable book, *Voices Prophesying War, 1763–1984*: 'Between 1871 and 1914 it was unusual to find a single year without some tale of future warfare appearing in some European country.'

But it is Wells's master stroke to have the invaders arrive from another planet! No communication, no truce, is possible. The appearance on the stage of the hideous Martians, with their bad habits, decidedly raises the stakes and gives the novel an almost mythopoeic strength.

The War of the Worlds begins with portents in the sky above a peaceful England, with people going about their daily business. What some believe to be a meteor lies half-buried in a pit on the sandy common near Woking. Some people have a look. They are mistaken. The supposed meteor is a cylinder, the top of which slowly unscrews. Onlookers gather. In Chapter 4, something emerges from the cylinder, something which 'glistened like wet leather' (p. 26). Wells makes sure we understand how repulsive the Martians are, without going into detail at this juncture.

A delegation waving a white flag approaches the cylinder. The men are determined to communicate with their alien visitors. The Martians turn a heat ray on the delegation. All are killed. Now we understand how remorseless the Martians are, lacking the qualities of emotion and empathy.

The narrator of the story is at first alarmed; but when he gets home and sits down to a good meal, his mood improves. He believes the Martians are terrified, saying, 'Perhaps they expected to find no living things – certainly no intelligent living things.'

People talk about the unusual event, but it does not make 'the sensation that an ultimatum to Germany would have done'. By similar touches, Wells brings verisimilitude to his tale.

A second cylinder arrives.

Soon the peaceful English countryside is burning. The Martians use their heat ray. Perhaps with a nod towards *The Battle of Dorking*, the military are slow to get into action. Things go steadily and satisfyingly from bad to worse. Church steeples tumble down. People hide in trenches and cellars. While composing this story, Wells was cycling round the area. 'I completely wreck and sack Woking — killing my neighbours in painful and eccentric ways,' says he, with a certain sadistic relish.

It is destructive. However, destruction was modish. The taste of ruination was not in the mouths of the home population. The Edwardians were as yet merely the children of a century in which a hideous adulthood was yet to come. So D.H. Lawrence exclaims in 1922, 'Three cheers for the inventors of poison gas', and 'Let all schools be closed at once', while T.S. Eliot regrets the spread of education, which is 'lowering our standards . . . destroying our ancient edifices'.

The nameless narrator witnesses the destruction of Weybridge and Shepperton. Always, the machines are contrasted with that essentially English invention, the countryside: 'The armoured Martians appeared, far away over the little trees, across the flat meadows that stretched towards Chertsey, and striding hurriedly towards the river.' And these machines take no more notice of the humans than would the humans of 'a confusion of ants'.

The narrator meets a curate. The curate, like the Artilleryman we meet later, is there merely to express a viewpoint; this is not really a characterization. But to my memory, the world of fiction was once populated with chinless wonders of vicars and curates; they were popular Aunt Sally figures – Aunt Sallys being popular recreational dummies in public house gardens, designed merely to have wooden balls shied at them.

Wells's curate is there to express the helplessness of organized religion when faced with the invaders. 'All the work – all the Sunday-schools – what have we done? The end! The great and terrible day of the Lord!' Etc. '"Be a man!", said I' (p. 70).

We learn that the narrator has a brother in London. The scene is thus enabled to shift to the city. Everything is calm there, a calm giving way gradually to excitement and anxiety. Fugitives begin to pour in from West Surrey. The Martians advance, and by Chapter 16 panic and disorder – how Wells hated disorder! – take over. There is 'a swift liquefaction of the social body' (p. 92).

We may ask ourselves today if something similar would take place, supposing al-Qaeda launched bombs containing anthrax upon the capital. I asked myself a similar question when, visiting the bookstall on Paddington station in the Second World War, I came upon a reprint of this novel;

the jacket showed searchlight beams in the sky and flames arising from the destroyed city. Some fears remain ever topical. The Martians are as remorseless as was the Luftwaffe.

It is not necessary to relate what happens next; we can safely leave that to Mr Wells. The question arises as to what was going on in the capacious mind of the author when he wrote about this wholesale destruction. The subject of colonialism emerges; the cruel treatment of the Tasmanians is mentioned. Wells was not alone in reflective mood. Rudyard Kipling's poem, 'Recessional', was published in 1897. It contains the line, 'Lo, all our pomp of yesterday is one with Nineveh and Tyre.'

More constantly on Wells's mind was the question of over-population – long before this became a subject for common discussion. Thomas Malthus's *An Essay on the Principle of Population* was published in the last years of the eighteenth century. Malthus points out that whereas population increases in a geometrical ratio, subsistence increases only in an arithmetical ratio. An increasing number of people will go hungry. Such is a rule of nature: 'And the race of man cannot, by any efforts of reason, escape from it. Among plants and animals, its effects are waste of seed, sickness, and premature death. Among mankind, misery and vice.'

Although this stern judgement has been somewhat ameliorated by crop development and improved agricultural methods, Malthus still rules. And, as John Ruskin says in *Unto This Last*, 'In all the ranges of human thought, I know none so melancholy as the speculations of political economists on the population question.'

Later, when his amazing creativity was on the wane, Wells in his didactic mode devoted whole books to the question of over-population. In his *A Modern Utopia*, 'degenerates' are prevented from breeding. The so-called idiots, drug addicts, drunkards, and violent men are exiled on various islands, and carefully policed.

Wells is, of course, one of the most prodigal producers of utopias. In book after book, society is overturned, eventually to develop a better and more orderly world. Perhaps we find such themes less convincing nowadays, after the ghastly regimes established in the middle decades of the last century. In 1910, some years after the publication of *The War of the Worlds*, Wells published the charming *History of Mr Polly*. While embodying many aspects of Wells's own earlier life, most notably Mr Polly's escape from drapery shops, the novel also contains a dream shared by many men of that time: escape from the captivity of shops to becoming a casual worker in a rural inn, owned by a pleasant woman and situated on the banks of an unsullied river. It is a form of one-man utopia, where Mr Polly finds happiness at last.

A pleasant variant on this scenario is played out in *Nineteen Eighty-Four*, where Orwell's humble notion of utopia is a private room and a girl to love. Mr Polly's utopia is of longer duration than that of Winston Smith. The mood had darkened by the 1940s.

This is a convenient place in which to say a word concerning some of the films and radio programmes made from Wells's book.

In October 1938, a radio play based on *The War of the Worlds*, starring Orson Welles, was broadcast in the United States (and re-broadcast much later on BBC radio). It was produced in documentary, the setting transposed to the Eastern Seaboard of the USA. Many people fell into a panic, believing they were actually being invaded by Martians, and headed for the traditional hills. It is difficult to see today how listeners could have been so gullible, but learned universities have written about and a film studio made a movie about what happened that night.

The War of the Worlds was filmed by George Pal/Paramount Productions and released in 1953. The opening is impressive. Sir Cedric Hardwicke, eminent member of the British contingent in Hollywood at the time, narrates much of the first paragraph of the novel against a starry background.

England gives way to southern California. Woking gives way to Los Angeles. A square-jawed actor and a blank-faced actress provide a love affair. While the dialogue is plodding, the boomerang-shaped Martian war machines are attractive. It's a noisy film, full of destruction.

As we have seen, Wells's cleric is contemptible. Director Byron Haskin transforms him into a heroic figure. Advancing towards the Martian front line, the heroic vicar chants, 'Yea, though I walk through the Valley of Death, I will fear no evil', when Pow! – he is wiped out.

An American TV series based on the Wells novel arrived on the small screen in 1988 and ran for forty-two episodes.

These films bear witness to a difference in British and American temperaments. The British like – or certainly did like – a pinch of melancholy to their dish, for flavour's sake. The Americans prefer triumphant individualism, such as was propagated in science fiction by the Robert Heinlein/Isaac Asimov/John Campbell group of writers. This preference was shown even more clearly by the reception of *The War of the Worlds* in the USA.

The novel was run as a serial in an American newspaper. Americans were not going to take the Martian invasion lying down. A journalist, by name Garrett P. Serviss, wrote a kind of sequel to Wells's novel, entitled *Edison's Conquest of Mars*. Thomas Edison invents anti-gravity and a disintegrating ray, and sets off with a whole fleet of spaceships to pulverize Mars. The evil Martians are wiped out. As is Wells's lesson in humility.

There were reasons other than Malthus's essay on population to make a thinking man of Wells's time somewhat down in the mouth. There was, for example, William Thomson, Lord Kelvin's remarks on entropy: 'Within a finite period of time past, the earth must have been, and within a finite period to come, the earth must again be, unfit for the habitation of man as at present constituted.'

Wells had already reported on those bleak last days of the human race in *The Time Machine*. Now he was commenting on other theories, such as the theory of Laplace and his nebular hypothesis, that Mars was an older world than ours.

In an article in a review published in 1896, Wells discusses the possibility of intelligent life on Mars, and states, 'There is no doubt that Mars is very like the Earth.' The statement was plausible before various NASA fly-bys had shown Mars to be a barren and inhospitable rock, bereft of life, bereft certainly of anything approaching intelligent bipeds or the umbrella-bearing public of Wells's day.

Wells was labouring under an illusion shared by many who took an interest in matters astronomical at that period. We now know Mars to be not senile, merely inclement. But Wells's view of Martian life is cleverly linked with that other great nineteenth-century discovery which preoccupied Wells and others (as it still preoccupies us in our century), Charles Darwin's theory of evolution.

Wells reserves a close description of Martian anatomy until the second chapter of Book Two. There we are treated to three pages of exposition, and a detailed description of the Martian's anatomy, opening with the sentence: 'They were, I now saw, the most unearthly creatures it is possible to conceive' (p. 124). After we have become thoroughly and scientifically disgusted, comes the cool remark, 'To me it is quite credible that the Martians may be descended from beings not unlike ourselves' (p. 127). After all, who knows what we may become? As Wells says,

'We men . . . are just at the beginning of the evolution that the Martians have worked out' (p. 129).

Moreover, another nasty trait of the alien invaders, to be revealed later in the book, has perhaps been developed from Darwin's statement in *The Origin of Species*. In the chapter entitled 'The Struggle for Existence', Darwin states, 'The action of climate seems at first sight to be quite independent of the struggle for existence; but in so far as climate chiefly acts in reducing food, it brings on the most severe struggle between the individuals . . . which subsist on the same kind of food.'

Undoubtedly, the colder climate of the Red Planet would intensify this struggle, as Wells understood.

We can see that *The War of the Worlds* is a compendium of many nineteenth-century concerns. Of course it is more than that, for those concerns are woven into an extraordinary and fascinating tale. It is the foundation stone for all alien invasion stories, whether in print or in the cinema. Following Wells's example, many other stories were to come where the world, or England at least, is laid waste. Among these are Conan Doyle's *The Poison Belt*, John Wyndham's *The Day of the Triffids*, John Christopher's *The Death of Grass*, J. G. Ballard's *The Wind from Nowhere*, Aldous Huxley's *Ape and Essence*, and my own *Greybeard*. The danger and interest in writing of such things is that, in defying 'common sense', one does not fall into common idiocy. Wells is adroit in such matters. But of this sub-genre, it is the unsympathetic Martians who wear the laurel crown.

Scientific romances and science fiction are generally considered to be remote from the author's experience. That
can never be the case; what we are fills the fictions we tell,
often without our realizing it. What lurks as fugitive in the
mind comes out clearly on paper. As Mary Shelley says in
her introduction to *Frankenstein; or, The Modern Prometheus*
(1818), 'Invention, it must be humbly admitted, does not
consist in creating out of the void, but out of chaos; the
materials must in the first place be afforded: it can give
form to dark, shapeless substances, but cannot bring into
being the substance itself.' This was true in Wells's case; he
had an ample stock of dark, shapeless substances.

We see this clearly in two instances. When the narrator
is trapped with the curate in a ruined house, we find
theirs is a filthy semi-subterranean entrapment. They are
confined to the scullery of the half-destroyed building. We
have here, unmistakably, a reconstruction of the scullery
of Atlas House in which, when Bertie Wells was a lad,
his mother slaved away years of her life. The squalor and
discomfort of that room remained with Wells. Wells, like
Orwell after him, knew that dirt has political significance.
We find that scullery described again in the novel, *In the
Days of the Comet*, in section III, Chapter 4 – described
with sorrow.

He depicts it in part as 'a damp, unsavoury, mainly
subterranean region . . . rendered more than typically dirty
in our case by the fact that into it the coal-cellar, a yawning
pit of black uncleanness, opened, and diffused small

129

crunchable particles about the uneven brick floor'. There his mother works, 'a soul of unselfishness'. 'And while she washes up I go out, to sell my overcoat and watch in order that I may desert her.' This sad place is employed in *The War of the Worlds* as a symbol, for kitchens are places where things are prepared for eating. As the curate discovers.

The Martians have invaded Earth for a good meal. The narrator-storyteller sits down to a good meal before getting into his tale. Wells had an obsession with food – with both eating and being eaten. You can, to adapt an old saying, take the man out of the kitchen but you cannot take the kitchen out of the man. Peter Kemp wrote an entire book about Wells's appetites, entitled *H.G. Wells and the Culminating Ape*. People in *The War of the Worlds* are depicted as being part of the food chain. The inhabitants of Woking flee 'as blindly as a flock of sheep' from the Martian fire, as from a cooking pot!

The second instance in which Wells's early experience informs his thinking shines an interesting light on his attitude towards society. Wells the socialist followed a good radical pedigree. Like William Godwin, he regarded humanity as perfectible; like Percy Bysshe Shelley, he believed in free love. Yet this socialist was never entirely on the side of his fellow men. He had little belief in the immutability of the social order. The Artilleryman, an unpleasant character, looks forward to the overturn of society. 'There won't be any more blessed concerts for a million years or so,' he says. 'There won't be any Royal

Academy of Arts, and no nice little feeds at restaurants'
(p. 154).

Wells in his youth had experienced a remarkable
example of social change which came about peacefully.
His mother, Sarah Wells, left his father and went to work
as housekeeper at Up Park, 'the big house' in Sussex.
Lady Fetherstonhaugh was the owner of Up Park. She had
started life as a milkmaid in the grounds, under the rather
apt name of Mary Ann Bullock. The lord of the manor
had taken a fancy to Mary Bullock; he packed her off to
Paris to be educated and refined, and then married her.
After his death, Lady Fetherstonhaugh ruled Up Park in
solitary splendour. She was a striking instance of the social
mobility which Wells himself achieved.

Despite frequent illness, Wells was a high-spirited chap.
At the least, he put on high spirits. His letters to his mother
and his friends are adorned with comic little sketches –
the 'picshuas', as he calls them. But as to the intellectual
aspect of the culture, there was much to depress a thinking
Victorian. Lord Kelvin had pronounced that the lump of
rock on which everyone lived would last only for another
20 million years. The death of the sun, in the days before
nuclear activity was understood, was also thought to be
comparatively and depressingly near. These were matters
dramatized in Wells's *The Time Machine*, published in 1895,
three years before *The War of the Worlds*.

It had once been the habit of many English novelists to
open their novel with the words, 'It was in the winter of

the year 18– . . .' or, 'Early in the reign of King William IV . . .'. These dates possibly signify a time when the author was young; things were assumed not greatly to have changed since that date. However, as the nineteenth century progressed, things were greatly changing. Gradually, novels crept into the present. Wells, in his impatience, starts his novel in – leaps into – the future.

Could this strange idea of setting novels in future time be a contributory factor for the way in which such novels are ruled out of court by a literary elite? Surely it is not only 'the masses' who think of the future as a proper dwelling-place for the imagination? In any case, Wells enjoyed a splendid creativity for the seven years from 1895 to 1901. The best of his science fiction (though not of his ordinary social fiction) was written then, and most of the stories are of social dissolution, of uncomfortable new worlds opening up, old worlds being bludgeoned down to their knees.

There is an argument which says that much of this mood is attributable to *fin de siècle* angst; I would rather attribute it, as Wells himself did, to a new way of thinking. In his brilliant discourse, 'The Discovery of the Future', delivered to the Royal Institution in 1902, he distinguishes between two divergent mental attitudes. He opens his speech by saying he wishes to 'contrast and separate two divergent types of mind, types which are to be distinguished chiefly by their attitude towards time'.

The predominant type scarcely thinks of the future. A much less abundant but more modern type 'thinks constantly and by preference of things to come, and of present things mainly in relation to the results that must arise from them'. Wells sees this type of person as 'perpetually attacking and altering the established order of things'. The pungent medicine so artfully infused throughout *The War of the Worlds* is designed to conscript more minds into the futurist category.

An older mistaken point of view was expressed by C.K. Shorter in 1897. 'The imagination is everything, the science is nothing; but the end of the century, which shares Mr Wells's smattering of South Kensington, prefers the two together; and I sympathise with the end of the century.'

Be that as it may, Wells's vivid imagination won the day. His success was assured, his poverty left behind. The destruction of a world that has become so dingy is perhaps Wells's way of living down the ugly world, the sordid scullery, from which he had escaped. He remains troubled nevertheless. His friend Arnold Bennett praises Wells for writing for 'the intelligent masses', in the days when intellectuals were against newspapers, as latterly they were against the cinema and then television and, in short, anything popular.

Such problems are well aired in John Carey's book, *The Intellectuals and the Masses*. He puts Wells's time and Wells's problems into context by quoting briefly from *Marriage* where Trafford speaks of a dyspeptic socialist in these terms: 'It seemed to him that in meeting Dowd he was meeting all that vast new England outside the range of ruling-class dreams, that multitudinous greater England, cheaply treated, rather out of health, angry, energetic, and now becoming intelligent and critical; that England which organised industrialism has created.'

Wells's problem was that he liked to consort with the great; yet he could not but remain an Outsider, a Steppenwolf, forever discontented. Carey well understands Wells's dilemma. As with today's science fiction writers, in general ring-fenced away from 'Literature'.

In 1901, Wells published his book of essays, *Anticipations*. Wells was listened to increasingly as a prophetic voice. He began to talk about the real world – as he saw it – rather than create more ingenious fantasies. The visionary novel, *In the Days of the Comet*, was published in 1906, and has never received the attention it deserves. It contains a harsh indictment of the ugliness of the world in which Wells grew up.

Wells, like Charles Dickens before him, became popular and successful in a way no contemporary writer could be, no Salman Rushdie, no Jeffrey Archer. He flew to Moscow to talk to Lenin and Gorki, he flew to Washington to talk to Roosevelt. Yet he was always an astringent writer, as *The War of the Worlds* shows. Nowadays, astringency is out of fashion in popular literature, more's the pity. It is the day of the feather-brained celebrity who serves as role model for the young – a case of the bland leading the bland.

How easily the end of *War* could have been a happy one, full of rejoicing at the defeat of an alien enemy. Instead, the chapter preceding the Epilogue is called 'Wreckage'. London seems to have become a city of tramps. Four weeks have gone by since the first cylinders landed. Mankind's view of a human future has been modified by the Martians. 'To them, and not to us, perhaps, is the future ordained' (p. 179).

The comment is justified. Humans are not victors but survivors. In comparison with the Martians, humans are a lesser breed. Unpleasant although the Martians are, they are intellectually our superiors. Unlike the Morlocks in *The Time Machine* or the Selenites in *The First Men in the Moon*, both of which groups live subterranean lives, the Martians come from 'above', the realms of the super ego.

In fact, the novel fizzes with metaphors which signify mankind's low estate. As we see, the very first paragraph of the book shows mankind and their affairs being studied much as a person with a microscope might scrutinize the creatures swarming in a drop of water.

We soon learn that the Martians have 'brightened their intellects, enlarged their powers and hardened their hearts'. In consequence, we who inhabit the Earth 'must be to them at least as alien and lowly as are the monkeys and lemurs to us' (p. 8).

When it comes to the exodus from London, Wells's fear of the fragility of civilization and his dislike of the masses is again in evidence.

135

All the railway lines north of the Thames [were choked], and the South-Eastern people at Canon Street had been warned by midnight on Sunday, and trains were being filled. People were fighting savagely for standing-room in the carriages even at two o'clock. By three, people were being trampled and crushed even in Bishopsgate Street, a couple of hundred yards or more from Liverpool Street station; revolvers were fired, people stabbed, and the policemen who had been sent to direct the traffic, exhausted and infuriated, were breaking the heads of the people they were called out to protect. (p. 92)

Undeniably, Wells had himself brightened his intellect, enlarged his powers, and hardened his heart. Yet we know there is another Wells, a playful man who invented brilliant games for boys (I played his 'Little Wars'), who spoke up for women's rights, who led a campaign in 1924 to save the whales. He was generous to other writers, he consorted with many women – who in general remained ever after friendly towards him. He enjoyed good company, good wine. He was a serious man, yet he was fun. The intelligentsia have never taken to Wells as a literary force.

I agree with the other members of the H.G. Wells Society in admiring, even loving, Wells. His son, Anthony West, says of Wells, 'Beyond that close circle of people who knew him, there was the larger army whose hearts were armed by the abundant spirit and courage which emanate from his writings and which make it easy to miss the intensity of his internal struggle with his demon.'

136

Wells said of himself, 'I fluctuate, I admit, between at the best a cautious and qualified optimism and my persuasion of swiftly advancing, irretrievable disaster.' We find him still so readable because we know in our hearts that the global disaster is still in progress.

If there is a conflict between his temperament as a man and as a writer – a conflict evident in many authors – one can only say that seated at a typewriter (how Wells would have relished the computer!) one knows for a certainty that one has, if not the best life, then one's very best choice of life. And what one pours out, alone in the room, is much like sessions of psychoanalysis, as one produces things that astonish even oneself.

A similar case is that of Emile Zola, of whom his biographer, F. W. J. Hemmings says that when Zola was writing, 'he passed into a totally different state of being: private terrors, dreams of ecstatic sensual delight, abominable visions of nightmarish intensity, took temporary possession of him'. It is not difficult to conjecture that the destruction of Woking released similar demons and energies in Wells.

That ghastly optimist, the Artilleryman, appears again, to announce that he and his kind will survive. They will live in London's drains and 'degenerate into a sort of big savage rat'. The passages regarding the Artilleryman were inserted by Wells after the serialization of his story. Perhaps he wished to have a mouthpiece who so starkly pronounced on the death of civilization; or, as some critics have suggested, Wells sympathized with this extremism. He also saw the world as too full of people, particularly those, as the Artilleryman states, who are 'useless and cumbersome and mischievous' (p. 157).

Most of those who flee the city meet with no compassion from Wells; they are likened to dodos, sheep, monkeys, and rats. People are fighting, being trampled, crushed, shot, and stabbed, or ploughed under by railway engines. The social body has liquefied, like liver under an attack of cancer. Sickness goes with the disorganization. Wells had a lifelong hatred of illness and disorganization. 'Martian sanitary science', we are told, 'eliminated illness ages ago. A hundred diseases, all the contagions and fevers of human life, consumption, cancers, tumours and such morbidities, never enter the scheme of their life.'

Here one recalls Joseph Conrad's old jibe at Wells, 'You don't care for humanity but think they are to be improved!'

One must admit that there is certainly room for improvement. And we remain grateful to H.G. Wells for pointing the matter out in this brilliant novel, so cogently, so memorably, so unsympathetically.

10

Thoughts on Science and Civilization

Thoughts on Science and Civilization

In one of my Oxford dictionaries, science is defined as 'an intellectual and practical activity which encompasses systematic study of the structure and behaviour of the physical and natural world through observation and experiment'. In other words, it requires study and hard work – and perhaps if we're lucky a glorious discovery which enlarges our understanding. Science aids us to appreciate the beauty and complexity of our planet, with the interlocking and cooperation of its myriad parts, which continue unceasingly, despite the concrete we pour over the grounds of the world. Science is an integral part of our civilization. Yet many civilized people, who bring up good families, who abhor the stoning of women and take functioning sewage systems for granted, are unaware of the great complexities of the universe in which we play a minor role.

Civilization, it seems, has a less confident definition: the stage of human social development and organization which is considered most advanced. Civilization must surely be comprehensive. It must include the containment of anger, the forbearance of condescension to others less fortunate than we, courtesy towards strangers and friends, a counterbalance of love and lust, the Himalayas, enjoyment of the seasons, and of the arts, and of all things that are themselves good, from Pinot Grigio to libraries, theatres, friendship, computers, and fresh air, combined with a lively interest in everything around us – together with an amazing lack of absorption in *Big Brother* . . . Oh, and a drive to quell global warming to save both civilization and our planet.

As a fairly civilized person, I believe that there was a point of origin of the universe, say at an unimaginable 14 billion years ago, when something was created from 'nothing' (I put the word in quotes because I am hard put to understand the words I am using), which expanded almost instantaneously into the universe in which we live.

We certainly know that the universe is still expanding. Science has discovered the fact. At that extraordinary beginning, matter and time exploded at a rate faster than light itself, to clot into suns and galaxies. The elements are born, among them carbon. So there was the possibility for 'life as we know it' to come about. Here we are, on this small planet, every living thing, composed of matter that must be infinitely old. So I believe, or at least attempt to believe. I do understand that something more or less like this must have occurred. Nor can I think of anything more wonderful. Yet I still celebrate Christmas. I still have affection and admiration for old English churches. Long before our modern care units, our modern hospitals, our modern understanding of life, death, and all the ailments in between, little churches covered the land, offering condemnation of bad behaviour, comfort, consolation, officiation over birth, marriage, old age, and death. They also offered – as they did when I was a boy – some fairy tales about God making the world in seven days, and offering sinners eternal damnation. And since it seems highly likely that life began in the ocean, bang goes that fairy tale about Adam and Eve in their – what was it now? – the Ocean of Eden?

* * *

Civilization is maintained by ordinary persons and advanced by extraordinary persons. There are visions that can greatly improve living standards. We must allow them the context in which they can breathe. Quite simple things, like stopping goats climbing trees, achieve beneficial effects.

Let me explain. Rajasthan is largely dry desert. In the sixteenth century, a wise man in a small impoverished village had a vision of better life for all. A few rules had to be obeyed. The man was dying, so his daughter wrote down her father's simple edicts:

> Goats must be tethered, so that they cannot eat saplings or climb and kill trees.

143

No tree should be cut down until at least a century old.

No family should have more than three children.

And similar ordinances. In a short while, the village became greener and the heat therefore less intense. Experiencing this improvement, the villagers observed the laws then and do so to this day. They live in a green environment. They are not greedy. They have aspired to live well. Some nearby villages have got the idea. They too prosper.

*   *   *

Yet Vision on its own, without other checks and balances, can lead to disaster. There is the case of the Indian king who was told by a wise man of his vision. He advised the king to build a splendid palace on the hills some distance away. The king was convinced. Slaves worked for many years to create the grand structure called Fatehpur Sikri. It was finished at last – and only then did they discover there was no source of water anywhere nearby. The palace – never lived in – remains to dazzle the eyes of tourists. They have to take their own bottled water. Water in a bottle is another product of civilization. Of course you have to pay for it . . .

*   *   *

Just as our world is mainly covered by ocean, so we find in it a great ocean of inequalities. I propose a litmus test. The degree of civilization a nation has achieved relates to the status and treatment of women. Those nations which stone women to death for adultery are not civilized. The men of such nations must be treated with scrutiny, if not suspicion. Despite talk of glass ceilings, Britain scores well here, to its benefit – though it is not so long since men were entitled to beat their wives for misbehaviour.

It does not do to be too pleased with ourselves. We have many prisons and many people crammed into those prisons. Some of those people have committed serious crimes; many are there because of ill chance, parental neglect or cruelty, poverty, ignorance, and/or misery. They need to acquire literacy if they lack it. They need compassion, understanding, comradeship, rather than iron bars. Low marks on the civilization scale here. And what, as Leo Tolstoy asked two centuries ago, entitles one man to punish others?

* * *

I have walked in villages overseas where the stink of sewage flowing in open ditches almost knocks you backwards. London smelt just as bad – just as bad, in fact, almost until the date when my father was born, in the last decade of the nineteenth century. The grand Victorian novels had been written by then, but it was not until the amazing Joseph Bazalgette got to work that the 'Great Stench' was defeated. Rates of cholera and typhoid declined at once.

Bazalgette imprisoned the outflow from open sewers in eighty-two miles of huge drains. The stinking River Fleet was imprisoned. Huge banks were built to house the final drainage system; now known as The Embankment. Heroic Bazalgette, a true apostle of civilization!

* * *

In fact, true civilization exists only in books. It is not practical. Utopias do not readily fall into the 'Do It Yourself' category. Thomas More's *Utopia* is the first utopia in the English tongue. It is of its time and suggests much that we may now find rather barbarous. For instance, More speaks of the cleanliness of his island: 'the filthiness and ordure of the streets is clean washed away within the running river'. There's a fine for doing that to the Mersey today. This aspiration tells us something about the Elizabethan city in which More lived.

* * *

Science and civilization are delicately balanced. They seem at present to change as rapidly as do our own lives. These days we are talking about iPods, biofuels, and recycling. You no longer require a roll of film for your camera. Or a camera itself. But if climate change becomes too advanced, the human race may perforce give up its brief tenure of the Earth. Perhaps nothing will remain but the stromatolites on deserted Australian beaches – those ancient structures which first introduced oxygen into Earth's atmosphere. All that we have achieved and failed to achieve will be gone.

146

Indeed, much may be going now. Just as every dog has its day, so has every empire. I refer to the phantom empire of the West, fuelled by oil and trade, and trade in arms. When the impending recession or depression – whichever you call it – goes away, it will leave behind it the ruins of banks and homes and great institutions. Alas, such is the nature of humankind, we all get what we can. A luxury cruise, a second home, a third home, jewellery, cars for our kids, computer games for our kids, an extra crate of wine. Need I go on? Yes, I do need. Someone from a poor country to wash and iron for us, or to tend our gardens, mend our roads.

*   *   *

My generation grew up in a depression, a depression that continued until the Second World War in 1939. Why did so many of us volunteer for the Armed Forces in the two world wars? Because we could be sure of a square meal every day.

After the War, in the drab years that followed, foodstuffs were rationed – bread until 1951. We have had to be parsimonious. Once we found you could get cash out of a slot even if the bank was closed, there was no stopping us. The magic slot, the credit card – wow! – we spent like there was no yesterday. For us the awful term 'retail therapy' was coined. We have spoiled ourselves into the present mess.

*   *   *

Sometimes revelation comes unexpectedly. I had no objection to being a soldier; after all, I had spent nine years at boarding and public school. After the Burma campaign, we were stationed near Calcutta. I was walking down Chowringhee, one of the main streets. I had a Sten gun over my shoulder and was clattering along in well-shod army boots. Around me were Indians. There was famine in Bengal at the time. These people were all thin, dressed simply in one long piece of cloth. They went quietly barefoot, their facial expressions calm, peaceful. It was then the bulletin arrived in my mind, 'We've got something wrong.'

It follows that happiness is a bit of good luck, often illusory. Sadness is realism. And there is something resembling sorrow, sturdier than sorrow, such as you find in old masters, such as Lucretius. And Socrates is reported as saying, 'It seemed to me a superlative thing, to know the explanation of everything, why it comes to be, why it perishes, why it is.' Socrates must have known that some advances are the result not solely of intention but of happy accidents.

For example, Dr Johnson spoke of 'the pernicious habit of drinking tea'. Cholera and dysentery were and are great spreaders of mortality. In the sprawling and filthy city of London in Johnson's day, the mid-eighteenth century, crowds passed on disease one to the other. The great Bazalgette was yet to be. One can imagine that a worshipper in his pew in a crowded church could well sit next to a stranger who might, by the freight in his breath when hymn-singing, or by itinerant bugs when kneeling in prayer, hasten his neighbour's arrival in heaven.

From Johnson's time onwards, dysentery was loosing its grip on English people. Tea-drinking had become a habit. Three cheers for the clippers of the British Empire! But it was not the leaves of the tea plant that proved so beneficial: the fact was that, to make a good cup of tea, you have to boil the water. Thus dangerous bacteria and other antibodies are stopped in their and our tracks.

* * *

Sometimes smiles of luck precede scowls of misfortune. Do we imagine that the first man to invent a sail to speed his dugout across the river was going to hesitate because the development of that little stretch of canvas would lead in the future to the Spanish Armada? When Mr Ford built his first car at the beginning of the last century, it beneficially rid the streets of horses and their dung. No one foresaw that cars would contribute their part to global warming in this century. We're ingenious, but the power of foresight has not been given us.

* * *

When the government abolished hanging – I was alive then – it was argued that abolition might lead only to more crime. But, on the whole, people were becoming less hardened to the dominance of pain. Can you imagine what agony it must have been to have a tooth pulled without anaesthetic – not to mention having a leg sawn off? Medicine was introducing ways of alleviating pain, which incidentally reinforced sensibilities. Parents would once say of their poor crying child, helpless in cot, or pram, or damp nappy, 'Let her have her cry out.' No one thought of comforting the child. It was callous. We don't think like that now, or so I hope. It is no mere coincidence that capital punishment was abolished in 1969. The communal mindset changed. And so parenting has become more complex – and we, it's hoped, more conscious of our failings as parents.

* * *

As genes transmit biological information, memes, according to Richard Dawkins, can be said to transmit ideas and belief information. Thus an idea may be developing that unifies concepts of religion and science. Our genes carry information; have they developed in a universe which itself carries, along with light and gravity, the possibilities for mind, the encryption of intelligence? If civilization holds, perhaps in another hundred centuries we shall have gained a better understanding of the matter.

11

Meeting Thomas Hardy

Meeting Thomas Hardy

This imaginary conversation with Thomas Hardy was written for a collection entitled *AfterWord: Conjuring the Literary Dead*. Each contributor was asked: If you could meet one deceased literary figure, who would that be? What would you ask? What would you say, and why? It was an opportunity to ignore the established facts and to indulge some personal fantasies and projections. Might asking questions and making connections from the vantage point of a more sophisticated age reveal more about the dead author or would it simply say something about Brian Aldiss?

Hardy was always fascinated by astronomy and the hugeness of the cosmos. He was an early post-Darwinian and frequently conceived of and wrote about supernatural forces that control the universe, more through indifference or caprice than any firm will. Yet he retained an emotional attachment with church rituals; this paradox runs through his work.

I hope that I might have touched upon questions that have seldom been asked, incidents that have been suppressed, or even thrown light on some of the secrets that have puzzled readers for years. But I must leave you to be the judge.

* * *

One day recently, I was walking along a dusty Wessex lane when I came to a church standing on the edge of a village. A figure was sitting on a folding stool, sketching the church. I stopped and spoke to him.

Although he was an old man with white hair and a wrinkled face, his eyes were bright, regarding me. He was evidently summing me up. He showed me his half-finished sketch, asking me what I thought of it. To be honest, I thought it pretty poor, but I strove to be complimentary.

He chuckled. 'It's not immensely good. That's one of the reasons driving me to become a writer.'

Then I realized I was conversing with Thomas Hardy, certainly one of the most famed English novelists of his time, certainly my favourite writer, certainly he from whom I had learnt many of the essentials of both prose and poetry.

Of course, I was paralysed. But he was wrapped up in his own concerns, frowning at his half-finished sketch. Then he said, without looking up, 'I am often reviled because I am an atheist. I do not believe in God, or in this nonsense about his son dying to redeem our sins, even two thousand-odd years after his death. Charles Darwin has done away with all that hocus-pocus. So you might wonder why I sit here, sketching a village church.'

I agreed it did seem odd.

'It's not odd at all,' he said. 'This church, and thousands of churches like it, represents not only religion but continuity, the continuity of English life and English tradition. That continuity which neither the upheavals of present-day thought, nor the building of the Great Western Railway in 1833, could destroy.'

'This will go onward, though dynasties pass,' I said, recalling a line from his poem, 'In Time of "The Breaking of Nations"'.

'I could not have put it better myself,' said Hardy, with a gleam of humour. As if glad to change the subject, he admitted that he preferred the writing of poems to the writing of novels. But it was a rule of life that one had to earn one's living. 'Why that should be a rule I am sure I don't know, but there it is. And then of course there's the lure of fame . . .'

'But you speak out for country life and humble folk.'

'I dined at the table of the Duke and Duchess of Devonshire only last evening,' he said, in a tone that held some reproof.

It was natural to wonder how the conversation might have gone at that distinguished table, and if it had consisted mainly of talk of fox hunting. As though he read my mind, he said, 'We adhered to problems of publication and verification. And we talked in general regarding the human pair.'

'You must have found that interesting.'

'Medium well,' he said, with some sharpness. He rose and stretched, closing his portfolio. Our conversation was ended. He nodded to me cordially enough and began to make his way toward the village. Talk of the human pair had upset Hardy, or at least it was not a subject on which he was prepared to embark with a stranger.

I went to the village pub and wrote down as much of that conversation with Hardy as I could remember. In our brief exchanges, he had mentioned Charles Darwin, whose funeral he had attended in his forties in 1882. In a recent biography of Hardy, Claire Tomalin's *Thomas Hardy: The Time Torn Man*, 2007, Darwin earns scarcely a mention, yet his findings are of major importance in the life of the writer. Darwin spelled out the mysterious labyrinths of terrestrial existence, working meticulously from such small items as the differing shapes of a bird's bill or the activities of earthworms. Such findings had emotional as well as intellectual power over Hardy; he felt an affinity with the great scientist, for he too was meticulous, he too was 'a man who used to notice such things' (to quote a line from his poem: 'Afterwards').

The pairings of humans from the darkness of the past, the human pair of man and woman today, had made Hardy uncomfortable and with some reason. He had been twice married and, by all accounts, neither pairing had been particularly happy. First, he had married Emma Gifford in 1874, and then, when Emma died in 1912, Florence Dugdale in 1914. And he was haunted by a third woman, the ghost of Emma Gifford; he seemed devoured by memories of her and possibly by his neglect of her, his coldness, which had cost them dear. It seems he became emotionally withdrawn from Florence; they hardly spoke – together yet apart in the dreary Max Gate in Dorchester, Dorset, where he lived from 1885, first with Emma and then with Florence, until his death in 1928.

Hardy's fame grew. At the beginning of the twentieth century, volumes of his verse began to pour out, from *Wessex Poems* in 1898 to *Winter Words* in 1928. His novel *The Trumpet-Major* apart, it was in these poems that I first encountered Hardy. I loved him, loved his pessimism, which so accorded with my own, loved his concern with love itself. His isolation was something I could share.

Fame provided some consolation for his disillusion. In 'A Hurried Meeting' he had written:

> You should have taken warning,
> Love is a terrible thing; sweet for a space
> And then all mourning, mourning . . .

Fortunately, this is not everyone's experience. Although, even as I sat at the table in the village pub, I overheard a trio of drinkers nearby laughing as one of them exclaimed, 'Women! – you can't live with 'em, can't live without 'em!' Hardy would have sympathized with the uncouth paradox.

157

Where Hardy would have won more general agreement lies in the difficulties that Charles Darwin's *Origin of Species* (1859) presented to a religious age, with its challenge to the authority of the Bible. In Hardy's grand series of novels, from *Under the Greenwood Tree* in 1872 to *Jude the Obscure* in 1895, we are treated to a tragic vision of a world full of pain – pain easily aggravated by human folly, or by the cruel accident of a love letter delivered, but going unnoticed because it was pushed under the door mat.

In his autobiography, written with Florence and published in 1928, he describes receiving a tribute on his eighty-first birthday from younger writers who wrote of 'the charity of your humour . . . sweetened by your sympathy with human suffering and endurance.' These good poets ignore Hardy's interest in the distant geological past and the vast distances of interstellar space, in both of which he seems to find cause for discomfort – the 'monsters of magnitude' being revealed by the rapidly unfolding science in his day. It was the imaginary Wessex that took, and still takes, the reader's fancy: the cottages, the Mellbridge choir, the milkmaids, the first threshing machine, and in general, the remembrance of things past, whether factual or otherwise.

The large, the small, did not escape Hardy's shrewd gaze. In that brilliant sonnet 'At a Lunar Eclipse', the question is asked how the great parades of history, 'nation at war with nation' are but shades compared with the immutable functions of the solar system. 'Is such the stellar gauge of earthly show?' he asks us.

That comparatively silly novel *Two on a Tower* treats of astronomy and the size of the galaxy in which we and Lady Constantine live and move and have our being. Up on that eponymous tower, the youthful Swithin endeavours to explain to Lady Constantine the monsters 'waiting to be discovered by any moderately penetrating mind.' She asks him what monsters he is talking about. 'Impersonal monsters, namely, Immensities,' he tells her. 'Until a person has thought out the stars and their interspaces, he has hardly learnt that there are things much more terrible than monsters of shape, namely, monsters of magnitude without known shape. Such monsters are the voids and waste places of the sky. Look, for instance, at those pieces of darkness in the Milky Way . . . Those are deep wells for the human mind to let itself down into.'

And, of course, he speaks even of the stars in terms of the transitory: 'These everlasting stars . . . they burn out like candles' (pp. 29–30; references are to the Penguin Classics edition).

As to the small, in *A Pair of Blue Eyes* comes the well-known passage when the lovers, Elfride and Knight, are in trouble. Knight has slipped over the cliff edge and hangs on desperately, while Elfride removes her underclothes to knot and make a rope from them with which to rescue him. Some early readers found this positively rude, and must have rushed at once to prayer, while more sophisticated readers applauded one particular aspect of Knight's dilemma as he hung there:

By one of those familiar conjunctions of things wherewith the inanimate world baits the mind of man when he pauses in moments of suspense, opposite Knight's eyes was an imbedded fossil, standing forth in low relief from the rock. It was a creature with eyes. The eyes, dead and turned to stone, were even now regarding him. It was one of the early crustaceans called Trilobites. Separated by millions of years in their lives, Knight and this underling seemed to have met in their place of death. It was the single instance within reach of his vision of anything that had ever been alive and had had a body to save, as he himself had now.

(A Pair of Blue Eyes, p. 200)

Hardy goes on to speak of the immense lapses of time before humankind appeared on the scene. 'They were grand times, but they were mean times too, and mean were their relics. He was to be with the small in his death.' Then comes the following sentence: 'Time closed up like a fan before him.' It is brilliant, Hardyesque, and consequently, startling.

Marcel Proust declared this rather trivial love story his favourite among Hardy's writings. I have often wondered if it was not Hardy's one sentence that started Proust on the road that led him to *Remembrance of Things Past* where time opens like a fan before us.

*　*　*

Looking through my set of Thomas Hardy's works, bound in the sombre green of Osgood, McIlvane & Co., 45

160

Albermarle Street, I decide that *The Return of the Native* is my favourite, even set against such competition as *Tess* and *Jude*, *The Woodlanders*, *The Mayor of Casterbridge*, with its overpowering first chapter, and *Far from the Madding Crowd*.

In *The Return of the Native*, Clim Yeobright, Eustacia Vye, Damon Wildeve, not forgetting Granfer Cantle, play out their drama on Egdon Heath.

The novel opens with a description of the heath toward the hour of twilight: 'The heaven being spread out with this pallid screen and the earth with the darkest vegetation, their meeting line at the horizon was clearly marked. In such contrast, the heath wore the appearance of an instalment of night which had taken up its place before its astronomical hour was come: darkness had to a great extent arrived hereon, while day stood distinct in the sky' (p. 9; references are to the Oxford World's Classics edition, 2005). Anyone who cannot respond to such perceptions is to be pitied. Nor is it merely description for description's sake. The coming of darkness, the onslaughts of time – such are constants in the encompassing heath of Thomas Hardy's cogitations, which will bring about the mayor's downfall.

In such passages, we catch a glimpse of the conscious oppressed by the unconscious, later to be christened 'The Immanent Will'. Hardy was always in conflict with himself; as he writes in his autobiography, 'half the time I believe . . . in spectres, mysterious voices, intuition, omens, dreams, haunted places, etc., etc. But then, I do not believe in these in the old sense of belief any more for that.'

The old sense of belief? Could that have died with the voyage of the *Beagle*?

Towards the end of the novel, Granfer Cantle — the novel's main well of humour — declares: 'In common conscience every man ought either to marry or to go for a soldier. 'Tis a scandal to the nation to do neither one nor t'other' (p. 382).

But Hardy goes deeper than either of these two alternatives, though both in fact are staples of his tragic theatre. They reappear in the historical work in which Earth is tortured by an overwhelming pattern of entropy, later to be called, as I have mentioned, the Immanent Will — this in the work that appeared toward the end of his life. This all-encompassing verse and prose drama, *The Dynasts*, is almost impossibly ambitious. It centres on one of Hardy's lifelong interests, the Napoleonic Wars. Even those who have not ventured into this vast and complex panorama, the English version of Tolstoy's *War and Peace*, may be familiar with the author's masterly piece of scene-setting. It must have influenced many a movie director.

> The nether sky opens, and Europe is disclosed as a prone and emaciated figure, the Alps shaping like a backbone, and the branching mountain chains like ribs, the peninsular plateau of Spain forming a head. Broad and lengthy lowlands stretch from the north of France across Russia like a grey-green garment hemmed by the Ural Mountains and the glistening Arctic Ocean.

For all his justified pride in the scope and variety of his poems, Hardy – as we see here – was a master of prose at a period when he strove, following the findings of Darwin and others, to express a new awareness of humanity's predicament.

The formidable *Dynasts* embraces an immense cast list, from Pitt and Fox, Nelson, the Empress Josephine, and Napoleon himself to heralds and soldiers. Even the women cowering beside the battlefields of Waterloo have their say. Above this great concourse fly phantom Intelligences, embodiments of the immensities spoken of previously by Swithin in his tower. Intelligences that comment on the war-torn scene of the planet below: the Spirit of the Years, the Spirit of the Pities, the Shade of the Earth. These are the invisible characters who open the drama, and who, in speech and verse, convey much of Hardy's thought and pain:

SHADE OF THE EARTH
What of the Immanent Will and Its designs?

SPIRIT OF THE YEARS
It works unconsciously as heretofore,
Eternal artistries in Circumstance,
Whose patterns, wrought by wrapt aesthetic rote,
Seem in themselves Its single listless aim,
And not their consequence.
(*The Dynasts*, Fore Scene)

Not to God, this great hymn, but the first to evolution.

12

Afterword:
The Other Hemisphere

Afterword:
The Other Hemisphere

Figure 1

We live as if we were one whole person. But a writer must be many phantom people in order to portray characters in a book or novel. All the strange ancient beings to be found in Robert Holdstock's Ryhope, in *Mythago Wood,* are in essence one person. We too have periods in our past when we know, looking back, we were strange ancient beings, possibly very different from our present selves.

The squiggle heading this section (Figure 1) is roughly based on a picture I made by copy and adaptation of a little picture, a doodle, that Tim, my son from my marriage with Margaret, drew and coloured by crayon when he was very young. I liked it so much I had to preserve it. Hence in its present form it is the work of two artists. This squiggle is its ghost.

The fore-part of our brains consists of two hemispheres, united by the corpus callosum. It seems as if the left-hand hemisphere is more adept at linear expression, that is, writing, while the right-hand hemisphere is better at handling the pictorial. I long ago decided I was favouring, or – let's be honest – overworking, my left-hand hemisphere. I had always had an intense interest in art, so I would exercise the other hemisphere, the right, more actively.

Descartes drew a weird diagram showing the influence of the soul on the brain (Figure 2). I was more involved with several artists, and their influence on me, in succession: G.B. Tiepolo, who moved me to write *The Malacia Tapestry*, de Chirico, Kandinsky, Bruegel, and,

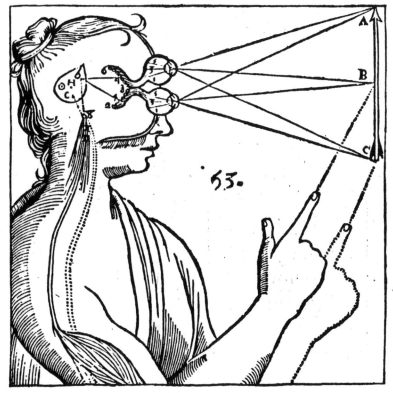

Figure 2

above all, Paul Gauguin. Gauguin at least provoked a poem. I valued Gauguin and his mysterious power above all. He knew sand was pink.

It follows – or possibly does not follow – that I have been absorbed in doing my own art stuff, mainly abstract, in watercolour, oils, pastel, or strips of coloured paper. I designed covers for some of my books, such as *Foreign Bodies*, *Life in the West*, *At the Caligula Hotel*, and, more recently, my book of selected poems, *Mortal Morning*. I came cheap. I never charged.

It was my kind family who suggested I should hold an exhibition in Oxford, to celebrate my eighty-fifth birthday. A hundred items went on display. Some sold. Some will soon be available as prints, in limited editions. I have discovered a new career! They asked me what I should call this exhibition. My immediate response: 'The Other Hemisphere'.

We create ourselves, for better or worse, or at least we create something metaphysical about ourselves. Let me give two examples, one operative in the art world, one in horticulture.

When I set out to create a colour abstract, I have, if not an idea, at least a drive to create. I get on the move. The colours guide me, or a shape; then I become sure of what I want. I surprise myself. It's much like the way in which one approaches a short story. Double gates seem to open in the mind, or in Descartes's soul. And of course some of these arrangements, these *isolées* of mine, are more effective than others.

When my second wife Margaret and I bought this present house, in what was to prove her final illness, I entirely reshaped the property, having all rotten and dangerous wiring ripped out, all bad plumbing replaced by new. The roof was insulated, and I had my builders add an extra third to the dimensions of the house, with a hall, an inner reception hall, a proper staircase, with spacious study and a bookroom added – these latter opening on to the lesser of two courtyards. When Margaret died, I, by no means a gardener, had to take over the garden, the wilderness. Cultivating the wilderness . . . It's what a writer does all the while.

A landscape gardener created two courtyards, lining them with old stone, one on either side of the house, plus a complex waterfall system. At the head of the waterfall sits Par Pri Mani, a Thai musician, piping his inaudible music.

Meanwhile, I set about creating the sort of garden I felt I needed, a garden with secret 'rooms', which comprise a Portuguese laurel, a long kolkwitzia hedge, two acers, a short avenue of cherry trees, grown from pips, also a small copse where hawthorns flower in spring. Fruit trees. And so on. Much else.

The assumption would be that this was work of one hemisphere or the other, but my belief is that the whole brain was articulating, an orchestration of a kind of art form I had never contemplated before. Now my patch is mysterious and mature and my delight, delighting others too.

I turned to Leo Tolstoy's book, *What is Art?* for this article. He writes that 'Art should make it so that the feelings of brotherhood and love of one's neighbour, now accessible only to the best people of society, become habitual feelings, an instinct for everyone.' I am not at all sure that my arts, such as they are, can do that. But at least Tolstoy considered the matter, knowing that art was important. He talks of beauty and religion in a nineteenth-century manner, whereas I would think of mystery or harmony. My garden represents harmony, as does Tim's and my little symbol.

As, one hopes, does the rest of this book.

References

1 Metaphysical Realism

Brian Aldiss, *Non-Stop*, London: Faber and Faber, 1958.
— *Greybeard*, New York: Harcourt, Brace and World, 1964.
— *Dark Light Years*, New York: Signet Books, 1964.
— *Report on Probability A*, London: Faber and Faber, 1968.
— *Frankenstein Unbound*, New York: Tor Books, 1973.
— *Harm*, London: Duckworth, 2007.
— *Walcot*, Rutland: Goldmark, 2009.
Stephen Hawking, *The Grand Design*, London: Penguin, 2010.
Anthony Storr, *The Dynamics of Creation*, New York: Scribner, 1972.

2 Paradise Square

Brian Aldiss, *Hothouse*, London: Faber and Faber, 1962.
— *Greybeard*, New York: Harcourt, Brace and World, 1964.

3 Hothouse

Percy G. Adams, *Travel Literature: The Evolution of the Novel*, Lexington: University Press of Kentucky, 1983.
Brian Aldiss, *Hothouse*, London: Faber and Faber, 1962.

Julian Huxley, 'The Meaning of Death', *Cornhill Magazine*, April 1911.

4 A Sight of Serbian Churches

Brian Aldiss, *Cities and Stones: A Traveller's Jugoslavia*, London: Faber and Faber, 1966.
— *Affairs at Hampden Ferrers*, London: Little, Brown, 2004.
Ivo Andrić, *The Bridge Over the Drina*, London: Harvill Press, 1994.
Rebecca West, *Black Lamb and Grey Falcon: A Journey through Yugoslavia*, London: Macmillan and Co., 1942.

5 Zulu

Note: I talk about two of the films adapted from my novels in this essay. The third was *Brothers of the Head* (2005) from my 1977 novel and directed by Keith Fulton and Louis Pepe.

Brian Aldiss, *Hothouse*, London: Faber and Faber, 1962.
— 'Super-Toys Last All Summer Long', *Harper's Bazaar*, December 1969.
— *Frankenstein Unbound*, New York: Tor Books, 1973.
Roger Corman, *How I Made a Hundred Movies in Hollywood and Never Lost a Dime*, New York: DaCapo Press, 1998.

6 The Ashgabat Trip

Brian Aldiss, *Somewhere East of Life*, London: Flamingo, 1994.

References

7 'It's the Disorientation I Relish'

Brian Aldiss, *Non-Stop*, London: Faber and Faber, 1958.

—— *Billion Year Spree: The History of Science Fiction*, London: Weidenfeld and Nicolson, 1973.

—— (ed.), *A Science Fiction Omnibus*, London: Penguin Classics, 2007 (originally published as *The Penguin Science Fiction Omnibus*, 1973).

George Basalla, *Civilized Life in the Universe: Scientists on Intelligent Extraterrestrials*, New York: Oxford University Press, 2005.

Edward Bulwer-Lytton, *The Coming Race*, London: Hesperus Press, 2007 (first published 1871).

John Clute (ed.), *The Encyclopaedia of Science Fiction*, London: Orbit Books, 1993.

Stephen Hawking, *The Grand Design*, London: Penguin, 2010.

Robert Holdstock, *Mythago Wood*, London: Gollancz, 2009 (first published 1984).

Ugo Malaguti (ed.), *Storia della Fantascienza*, Bologna: Perseo Libri, 1990.

Olaf Stapledon, *Star Maker*, London: Gollancz, 1999 (first published 1937).

Pierre Versins (ed.), *Encyclopédie de l'Utopie des Voyages Extraordinaires et de la Science Fiction*, Lausanne: L'Age d'Homme, 1972.

Mary Warnock, *Imagination*, London: Faber and Faber, 1976.

Fay Weldon, *The Cloning of Joanna May*, London: Flamingo, 1995 (first published 1989).

8 The Gulag Archipelago

Lesley Blanch, *The Sabres of Paradise: Conquest and Vengeance in the Caucasus*, London: Tauris Parke Paperbacks, 2004.

Robert Conquest, *The Great Terror: A Reassessment*, London: Pimlico, 2008.

Michael Scammell (ed.), *The Solzhenitsyn Files: Secret Soviet Documents Reveal One Man's Fight against the Monolith*, Chicago: Edition Q, 1995.

Alexander Solzhenitsyn, *The Gulag Archipelago*, translated by Thomas P. Whitney and Harry Willetts, London: The Folio Society, 2005.

9 The Continuing War of the Worlds

Brian Aldiss, *Greybeard*, Harcourt, Brace and World, 1964.

J.G. Ballard, *The Wind from Nowhere*, New York: Berkley Publishing, 1962.

John Carey, *The Intellectuals and the Masses: Pride and Prejudice Among the Literary Intelligentsia 1880–1939*, London: Faber and Faber, 1992.

John Christopher, *The Death of Grass*, London: Penguin Modern Classics, 2009.

I.F. Clarke, *Voices Prophesying War, 1763–1984*, Oxford: Oxford University Press, 1966.

Arthur Conan Doyle, *The Poison Belt*, New York: Cosimo Classics, 2008.

T.S. Eliot, *Notes Towards the Definition of Culture*, London: Faber and Faber, 1948.

F.W.J. Hemmings, *The Life and Times of Emile Zola*, New York: Scribner, 1977.

Aldous Huxley, *Ape and Essence*, London: Chatto and Windus, 1949.

Peter Kemp, *H.G. Wells and the Culminating Ape*, London: Macmillan, 1982.

References

D.H. Lawrence, *Fantasia of the Unconscious*, New York: Thomas Seltzer, 1922.

Garrett P. Serviss, *Edison's Conquest of Mars*, Burlington: Apogee Books, 2005.

H.G. Wells, *Anticipations*, Standard Publications, 2008 (first published 1901).

— *The First Men in the Moon*, London: Penguin Classics, 2005 (first published 1900).

— *The History of Mr Polly*, London: Penguin Classics, 2005 (first published 1910).

— *In the Days of the Comet*, London: Hogarth, 1985 (first published 1906).

— *Marriage*, London: Hogarth, 1986 (first published 1912).

— *A Modern Utopia*, London: Penguin Classics, 2005 (first published 1905).

— *The Time Machine*, London: Penguin Classics, 2005 (first published 1895).

— *The War of the Worlds*, London: Penguin Classics, 2005 (first published 1898).

John Wyndham, *The Day of the Triffids*, London: Penguin Modern Classics, 2001 (first published 1951).

10 Thoughts on Science and Civilization

Thomas More, *Utopia*, London: Penguin Classics, 2004.

11 Meeting Thomas Hardy

Thomas Hardy, *Wessex Poems*, Teddington: The Echo Library, 2008 (first published 1898).

— *Winter Words,* London: Macmillan and Co., 1928.

— *The Trumpet Major*, London: Penguin Classics, 2006 (first published 1880).

— *Human Shows Far Phantasies, Songs and Trifles*, London: Macmillan and Co., 1925.

— *Under the Greenwood Tree*, Oxford: Oxford World's Classics, 2009 (first published 1872).

— *Jude the Obscure,* Oxford: Oxford World's Classics, 2008 (first published 1895).

— *Two on a Tower*, London: Penguin Classics, 1996 (first published 1882).

— *A Pair of Blue Eyes,* Oxford: Oxford World's Classics, 2005 (first published 1873).

— *The Return of the Native*, Oxford: Oxford World's Classics, 2005 (first published 1878).

— *Tess of the d'Urbervilles*, Oxford: Oxford World's Classics, 2008 (first published 1891).

— *The Woodlanders*, Oxford: Oxford World's Classics, 2009 (first published 1887).

— *The Mayor of Casterbridge*, Oxford: Oxford World's Classics, 2008 (first published 1886).

— *Far From the Madding Crowd*, Oxford: Oxford World's Classics, 2008 (first published 1874).

— *Thomas Hardy* (with Florence Hardy), Ware: Wordsworth Editions Ltd, 2007 (first published 1928 and 1930 in two volumes).

— *The Dynasts*, New York: Macmillan, 1965 (first published in three parts, 1904, 1906 and 1908).

Dale Salwak (ed.), *AfterWord: Conjuring the Literary Dead*, Iowa City: University of Iowa Press, 2011.

Claire Tomalin, *Thomas Hardy: The Time Torn Man*, London: Penguin, 2007.

References

12 Afterword: The Other Hemisphere

Brian Aldiss, *The Malacia Tapestry*, London: Jonathan Cape, 1976.

—— *Foreign Bodies*, Singapore: Chopmen Publishers, 1981.

—— *At the Caligula Hotel*, London: Sinclair-Stevenson, 1995.

—— *Life in the West*, London: Abacus, 1998.

—— *Mortal Morning*, London: Flambard Press, 2010.

Robert Holdstock, *Mythago Wood*, London: Gollancz, 2009 (first published 1984).

Leo Tolstoy, *What is Art?* London: Penguin Classics, 2004.

PostScript
Books by mail since 1987

With novels and children's titles, and non-fiction including art, history and travel, you'll be surprised at what you might find among our discounted books.

Amazing deals on a wide range of books

Clearance

Bognor and Other Regises

King Arthur's alleged birthplace at Tintagel; palaces and castles; the Royal Oak at Boscobel – Caroline Taggart presents an overview of Britain's history through 100 royal locations.

publ £14.99 now £5.99
sale £2.99
Condition: New

Clearance

I Like Birds

This introduction to sixty British bird species offers anecdotes and information on their habitat, behaviour, features and song, paired with bold, stylized artwork.

publ £12.99 now £6.99
sale £4.99
Condition: New

Clearance

Slow Train to Guantanamo

From Havana to Guantanamo, award-winning foreign correspondent Peter Millar journeys through Cuba aboard a decaying railway system, sharing anecdotes, life stories and political opinions.

publ £11.99 now £5.99
sale £3.99
Condition: Very Good

Visit psbooks.co.uk/clearance today to find your next favourite read

Order line: 01626 897100 (8am–6pm, Mon–Fri)

For further information on the condition of our clearance books visit the FAQs section on our website – psbooks.co.uk/faqs

recycle
Or give me to a friend